I0448645

September 2013

DEPARTMENT OF HOMELAND SECURITY

Opportunities Exist to Better Evaluate and Coordinate Border and Maritime Research and Development

GAO-13-732

GAO Highlights

Highlights of GAO-13-732 a report to congressional requesters

DEPARTMENT OF HOMELAND SECURITY

Opportunities Exist to Better Evaluate and Coordinate Border and Maritime Research and Development

Why GAO Did This Study

Conducting border and maritime R&D to develop technologies for detecting, preventing, and mitigating terrorist threats is vital to enhancing the security of the nation. S&T, the Coast Guard, and DNDO conduct these R&D activities and S&T has responsibility for coordinating and integrating R&D activities across DHS. The Centers of Excellence are a network of university R&D centers that provide DHS with tools, expertise, and access to research facilities and laboratories, among other things. GAO was asked to review DHS's border and maritime R&D efforts.

This report addresses (1) the results of DHS border and maritime security R&D efforts and the extent to which DHS has obtained and evaluated feedback on these efforts, and (2) the extent that DHS coordinates its border and maritime R&D efforts internally and externally with other federal agencies and the private sector. GAO reviewed completed and ongoing R&D project information and documentation from fiscal years 2010 through 2013 and interviewed DHS component officials, among other actions.

What GAO Recommends

GAO recommends that DHS S&T establish timeframes and milestones for collecting and evaluating feedback from its customers to determine the usefulness and impact of its R&D efforts, and ensure that potential challenges with regard to data reliability, accessibility, and availability are reviewed and understood before approving Centers of Excellence R&D projects. DHS concurred with GAO's recommendations.

View GAO-13-732. For more information, contact David Maurer at (202) 512-9627 or maurerd@gao.gov.

What GAO Found

Between fiscal years 2010 and 2012, the Department of Homeland Security's (DHS) border and maritime research and development (R&D) components reported producing 97 R&D deliverables at an estimated cost of $177 million. The type of border and maritime R&D deliverables produced by DHS's Science and Technology (S&T) Directorate, the Coast Guard, and the Domestic Nuclear Detection Office (DNDO) varied, and R&D customers we met with reported mixed views on the impact of the R&D deliverables they received. These deliverables were wide-ranging in their cost and scale, and included knowledge products and reports, technology prototypes, and software (as shown in the figure below). The Coast Guard and DNDO reported having processes in place to collect and evaluate feedback from its customers regarding the results of R&D deliverables. However, S&T has not established timeframes and milestones for collecting and evaluating feedback from its customers on the extent to which the deliverables it provides to DHS components—such as US Customs and Border Protection (CBP)—are meeting its customer's needs. Doing so could help S&T better determine the usefulness and impact of its R&D projects and deliverables and make better-informed decisions regarding future work

DHS has taken actions and is working to develop departmental policies to better define and coordinate R&D, but additional actions could strengthen internal and external coordination of border and maritime R&D. S&T's Borders and Maritime Security Division, the Coast Guard, and DNDO reported taking a range of actions to coordinate with their internal DHS customers to ensure, among other things, that R&D is addressing high priority needs. However, work remains to be done at the agency level to ensure border and maritime R&D efforts are mutually reinforcing and are being directed towards the highest priority needs. For example, officials from university centers of excellence reported difficulties in determining DHS headquarters contacts, and officials from the primary land-border security R&D center reported delayed and cancelled projects due to the inability to obtain data. DHS could help ensure that the approximately $3 million to $4 million a year dedicated to the university Centers of Excellence is used more effectively by more carefully considering potential challenges with regard to data needs, access issues and data limitations before approving projects.

Examples of DHS S&T and Coast Guard Border and Maritime R&D Projects

Source: GAO.

Mobile Surveillance System Imager/Radar Upgrade, a retrofit kit developed by S&T BMD for CBP tested at the Arizona-Mexico border.

Source: USCG.

Shipboard Vessel Entanglement System developed by the Coast Guard and others for use on Coast Guard vessels.

_____ **United States Government Accountability Office**

Contents

Figures

Abbreviations

ASP	Advanced Spectroscopic Portal
BMD	Borders and Maritime Security Division
CBP	U.S. Customs and Border Protection
CIMES	Center for Island, Maritime, and Extreme Environment Security
COE	Centers of Excellence
COTS	commercial off-the-shelf
DHS	Department of Homeland Security
DNDO	Domestic Nuclear Detection Office
DOD	Department of Defense
DOE	Department of Energy
IV&V	Independent Verification and Validation
MARLIN	Multi-modal Automated Resolution, Location, and Identification of Nuclear Material
MIREES	Center for Maritime, Island and Remote and Extreme Environment Security
MSS	Mobile Surveillance System
NCBSI	National Center for Border Security and Immigration
NOAA	National Oceanic and Atmospheric Administration
OMB	Office of Management and Budget
OTIA	Office of Technology Innovation and Acquisition
PI	principal investigator
R&D	research and development
RDT&E	Research, Development, Test, & Evaluation
RPM	radiation portal monitor
S&T	Science and Technology
SIMON	Smart Integration Manager Ontologically Networked
SMS	Sensor Management System
SNM	special nuclear material
SQUID	Safe Quick Undercarriage Immobilization Device
TARD	Transformational and Applied Research Directorate
USCG	U.S. Coast Guard
WMD	weapons of mass destruction

GAO

U.S. GOVERNMENT ACCOUNTABILITY OFFICE

441 G St. N.W.
Washington, DC 20548

September 25, 2013

The Honorable Lamar Smith
Chairman
Committee on Science, Space, and Technology
House of Representatives

The Honorable Ralph M. Hall
House of Representatives

Conducting border and maritime research and development (R&D) to deliver technologies for detecting, preventing, and mitigating terrorist threats is vital to enhancing the security of the nation. The Department of Homeland Security (DHS) conducts research, development, testing, and evaluation of new technologies that are intended to achieve a range of homeland security goals, including detecting and preventing the unauthorized entry of persons or contraband into the United States; preventing and responding to nuclear, biological, explosive, and other types of attacks; and securing U.S. ports and inland waterways. DHS's Science and Technology (S&T) Directorate, the U.S. Coast Guard, and the Domestic Nuclear Detection Office (DNDO) conduct these R&D activities, although S&T has overall responsibility for coordinating and integrating R&D activities across DHS.[1] S&T funding for R&D grew steadily until 2010 and has served a wide variety of research areas. S&T also carries out R&D through its Office of University Programs, which manages and coordinates 12 University Centers of Excellence. The Centers of Excellence are a network of university R&D centers that provide DHS with tools, technologies, subject matter expertise, and access to laboratories and research facilities, among other things. Recently, Congress and others have raised questions about S&T's ability to demonstrate the impact of its investments—in terms of value, tangible products, and advances to the homeland security mission—as well as questions about the extent to which S&T is leveraging R&D already under way in the private sector and at other governmental agencies, including the Department of Defense. Accordingly, Congress has directed S&T to

---

[1]Homeland Security Act of 2002, Pub. L. No. 107-296, § 302,116 Stat. 2135, 2163-64 (codified as amended at 6 U.S.C. § 182).

GAO-13-732 DHS Border and Maritime R&D

demonstrate how its R&D efforts are timely, with results well defined, and based on clear and sensible priorities.[2]

In September 2012, we reported that DHS did not have a department-wide policy defining R&D or guidance directing its components how to report R&D activities.[3] As a result, DHS did not know its total annual investment in R&D, which limited the department's ability to oversee components' R&D efforts and align them with agency-wide R&D goals and priorities. We also reported that DHS's R&D efforts were fragmented and overlapping, which increased the risk of unnecessary duplication. Specifically, DHS had not developed a policy defining who was responsible for coordinating R&D and what processes should be used to coordinate it, and did not have mechanisms to track all R&D activities at DHS that could help prevent overlap, fragmentation, or unnecessary duplication. We recommended that DHS develop policies and guidance for defining, reporting and coordinating R&D activities across the department, and that DHS establish a mechanism to track R&D projects. DHS agreed with these recommendations and planned to make decisions about how to address these actions by May 2013. As of August 2013, DHS had not made a decision about how it specifically plans to address these recommendations.

In addition to our work on R&D across DHS, we have also reported extensively on the challenges that DHS has faced in deploying technologies and infrastructure to secure U.S. land borders and the maritime sector.[4] These continued challenges highlight the importance of effectively conducting, testing, and evaluating R&D technologies before they are transitioned to the customers who will operationally deploy them. For example, in November 2011, we reported on the U.S. Customs and Border Protection's (CBP) technology deployment plan for the Arizona border—the Arizona Border Surveillance Technology Plan—which was expected to cost approximately $1.5 billion over 10 years.[5] Specifically,

---

[2]H.R. Rep. No. 112-91, at 126-27 (2011).

[3]GAO, *Department of Homeland Security: Oversight and Coordination of Research and Development Should Be Strengthened*, GAO-12-837 (Washington, D.C.: Sept. 12, 2012).

[4]GAO, *Border Security: DHS's Progress and Challenges in Securing U.S. Borders*, GAO-13-414T (Washington, D.C.: Mar. 14, 2013).

[5]GAO, *Arizona Border Surveillance Technology: More Information on Plans and Costs Is Needed before Proceeding*, GAO-12-222 (Washington, D.C.: Nov. 4, 2011).

GAO-13-732 DHS Border and Maritime R&D

we reported that CBP did not have the information needed to fully support and implement the technology deployment plan in accordance with DHS and Office of Management and Budget guidance. Further, in September 2010, we reported on the challenges DHS faced in its efforts to test, evaluate, and operationalize maritime container security technologies.[6] We have also reported on DHS's efforts and challenges in developing technologies—such as sensors and transponders—capable of detecting and tracking small vessels in ports, technologies for detecting and reporting intrusions into and the tracking of cargo containers as they pass through the global supply chain, and the scanning of cargo through advanced automated radiography systems.[7]

As the result of past technology challenges and questions about the extent to which border and maritime R&D investments are being overseen and coordinated effectively across DHS, you requested that we review DHS's border and maritime R&D efforts. Accordingly, this report addresses the following two questions:

1. What have been the results of DHS's border and maritime security R&D and to what extent has DHS obtained and evaluated feedback on these efforts?

2. To what extent does DHS coordinate its border and maritime R&D efforts internally (with other DHS components and end users) and externally with other federal agencies and the private sector?

To answer the first objective, we focused our review on the components and offices receiving direct R&D appropriations related to border and maritime security—specifically, DHS S&T, the Coast Guard, and DNDO. To determine the results of DHS's recent R&D efforts, we asked officials from each R&D office to identify the deliverables their offices produced from fiscal years 2010 through 2012, including the cost of each deliverable. We corroborated the DHS-identified lists of deliverables and their costs with varied documentary evidence, including congressional budget justifications, DHS materials prepared for independently produced R&D reviews, and other published material. We determined that the

---

[6]GAO, *Supply Chain Security: DHS Should Test and Evaluate Container Security Technologies Consistent with All Identified Operational Scenarios to Ensure the Technologies Will Function as Intended*, GAO-10-887 (Washington, D.C.: Sept. 29, 2010).

[7]GAO, *Maritime Security: Responses to Questions for the Record*, GAO-11-140R (Washington, D.C.: Oct. 22, 2010).

information on deliverables and costs was sufficiently reliable for the purposes of providing an overview of Border and Maritime R&D; limitations to the data are noted in the report. For each component, we selected deliverables to reflect a range of product types and recipients and then asked DHS to identify the customers that received those deliverables. For the purposes of this report, we relied on DHS to identify who its customers were—in other words, those agencies that worked closest to S&T over the course of a project. We also refer to the reports, prototypes, software, or other project outputs as R&D deliverables. We selected these definitions because they are in keeping with those used by S&T. Given that S&T, the Coast Guard, and DNDO have different roles with respect to conducting and managing R&D, we selected different numbers of deliverables to review within each component. Specifically, given S&T's role as the lead R&D agency for DHS and its wider variety of customers, we interviewed every customer of S&T Border and Maritime Security Division's identified deliverables (20 of 20 deliverables). We met with 35 percent of the customers of the Coast Guard's completed deliverables (8 of 23 deliverables) and 12 percent of the customers of DNDO's deliverables (5 of 42 deliverables, which included one discontinued project). We met with fewer DNDO customers because the majority of DNDO's R&D projects are merged into new or continuing DNDO R&D efforts. Further, these efforts do not transition to customers outside of DNDO. In other words, DNDO's R&D customers were other DNDO R&D offices, and accordingly, we selected a smaller number of these DNDO project managers for follow-up. To corroborate customer views on the effectiveness, timeliness, and other aspects of the deliverables, we interviewed multiple customers per deliverable where possible and also validated customer views with the relevant DHS project managers where possible. Further, we evaluated DHS's efforts to assess the impact of its R&D against selected best practices from the National Academy of Sciences for evaluating the relevance and impact of R&D and best practices for project management.[8]

To evaluate DHS's ongoing R&D efforts, we met with S&T Borders and Maritime Security officials and Coast Guard, DNDO, and S&T Office of University Programs officials. We corroborated information received on

---

[8]National Academy of Sciences, "*Best Practices in Assessment of Research and Development Organizations.*" The National Academies Press, (Washington, D.C.: 2012). Project Management Institute, *A Guide to the Project Management Body of Knowledge (PMBOK® Guide), Fifth Edition,* (Newton Square, PA: 2013).

DHS R&D efforts through interviews with CBP (including the Office of Technology Innovation and Acquisition, Office of Border Patrol, Office of Air and Marine, Office of Information and Technology, and Office of Field Operations) and interviews with officials from three DHS University Centers of Excellence. Further, we conducted site visits to the Coast Guard's Research and Development Center in New London, Connecticut; CBP's Office of Border Patrol's Tucson Sector, Arizona; and one of DNDO's research contractors in North Billerica, Massachusetts, to observe and discuss DHS R&D projects and R&D results. The results of the site visits are not generalizable to all R&D projects, but provided important observations and insights into border and maritime R&D efforts across three different components. To address the second objective, we used the information we gathered above and insights from our interviews with DHS components, R&D project managers, and R&D customers to identify how DHS coordinates its R&D efforts internally, externally, on a per-project basis, and with the private sector. We compared these efforts with DHS's strategic plans, project management plans, and other published guidance related to coordination, as well as with best practices for coordination among federal agencies and best practices for effective evaluation design.[9] To evaluate DHS's efforts to conduct and coordinate R&D with its university research partners, we interviewed five universities representing three DHS Centers of Excellence that conduct border and maritime R&D—including a site visit to the University of Arizona, Tucson.

We conducted this performance audit from August 2012 through September 2013 in accordance with generally accepted government auditing standards. Those standards require that we plan and perform the audit to obtain sufficient, appropriate evidence to provide a reasonable basis for our findings and conclusions based on our audit objectives. We believe that the evidence obtained provides a reasonable basis for our findings and conclusions based on our audit objectives.

---

[9]GAO, *Results-Oriented Government: Practices That Can Help Enhance and Sustain Collaboration among Federal Agencies*, GAO-06-15 (Washington D.C.: Oct. 21, 2005), and GAO, *Designing Evaluations: 2012 Revision*, GAO-12-208G (Washington, D.C.: 2012).

Background

DHS Border and Maritime R&D Roles, Responsibilities, and Processes

S&T BMD

The Borders and Maritime Security Division is one of six technical divisions within S&T. It works to provide technical solutions to DHS operating components, such as CBP, in order to secure U.S. air, land, and maritime boundaries, including U.S. ports of entry, vast stretches of remote terrain, and inland waterways. BMD funds, directs, and manages the research, development, prototyping, and test and evaluation of technical solutions for border, maritime, and cargo security.

Below: tunnel with lighting, ventilation, and full standing headroom.

Source: DHS.

Within DHS, three components have responsibilities for conducting border and maritime R&D—S&T, the Coast Guard, and DNDO. S&T has five technical divisions responsible for managing the directorate's R&D portfolio and coordinating with other DHS components to identify R&D priorities and needs.[10] The Borders and Maritime Security Division (BMD) is responsible for most of S&T's border and maritime related R&D, and its primary DHS customer is CBP. Most of S&T's R&D portfolio consists of applied and developmental R&D, which is R&D that can be transitioned to use within 3 years, as opposed to longer-term basic research.[11] In addition to conducting projects for its DHS customers, S&T conducts projects for other federal agencies and first responders.

The S&T Office of University Programs also manages the DHS Centers of Excellence, which constitute a network of universities that conduct research for DHS component agencies on topics ranging from animal disease defense to catastrophic event preparedness.[12] Of the nine funded centers, two are dedicated to border and maritime R&D—The National Center for Border Security and Immigration (NCBSI), led by the University of Arizona in Tucson and the University of Texas at El Paso, and the Center for Maritime, Island and Remote and Extreme Environment

---

[10]These divisions are the Borders and Maritime Division, the Chemical/Biological Defense Division, the Cyber Security Division, the Explosives Division, and the Resilient Systems Division (which was formerly two separate divisions–Human Factors and Infrastructure Protection and Disaster Management).

[11]As defined by the Office of Management and Budget (OMB) (OMB Circular No. A-11 Section 84), basic research is a systematic study directed toward a fuller knowledge or understanding of the fundamental aspects of phenomena and of observable facts without specific applications toward processes or products in mind. Applied research is a systematic study to gain knowledge or understanding to determine the means by which a recognized and specific need may be met. Developmental research is a systematic application of knowledge or understanding, directed toward the production of useful materials, devices, and systems or methods, including design, development, and improvement of prototypes.

[12]The centers were established by the Homeland Security Act of 2002, as amended (6 U.S.C. § 188(b)(2)(A)), which states, "The Secretary, acting through the Under Secretary for Science and Technology, shall designate a university-based center or several university based centers for homeland security. The purpose of the center or these centers shall be to establish a coordinated, university-based system to enhance the Nation's homeland security."

S&T University Programs—Centers of Excellence

Each center is university-led or co-led in collaboration with partners from other institutions, agencies, national laboratories, think tanks, and the private sector.

Below: unmanned port security vessel.

Source: University of Hawaii.

Coast Guard

The Coast Guard's Research, Development, Test and Evaluation (RDT&E) program supports the Coast Guard's various missions by helping transition new technologies into the service's operational forces. The program is composed of the Office of RDT&E near Coast Guard headquarters in Washington, D.C., and the Research and Development Center (RDC) at New London, Conn.

Below: Coast Guard Biometrics Identification.

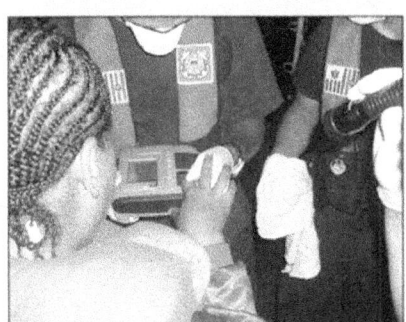

Source: USCG.

Security (MIREES), led by the University of Hawaii and Stevens Institute of Technology.[13] Centers are typically funded through cooperative agreements for 5-to-6 year periods, with a review period each year.[14] Ideas for projects to be undertaken by the centers are solicited at technical workshops with component-level subject matter experts, where the centers and DHS officials discuss technical or informational challenges. The Office of University Programs drafts these topics into research questions which the Office publishes in a funding opportunity announcement. The Office of University Programs then examines proposals it receives based on how the research could potentially further DHS's mission. Centers also hold annual meetings where officials are expected to brief DHS leadership on their work and their plans. Additionally, DHS stakeholders will give presentations on their technology needs and challenges. The centers are then expected to incorporate these needs and challenges into their programs.

The Coast Guard is a multimission, maritime military service within DHS.[15] The Coast Guard's R&D efforts are conducted and managed by its Research, Development, Test, & Evaluation (RDT&E) Program, which consists of the Office of RDT&E and the Research and Development Center. The center performs research, development, testing, and evaluation in support of all Coast Guard missions, as required.[16] The majority of the Coast Guard's R&D products are knowledge products, such as acquisition analysis studies or technical reports, as opposed to

---

[13]Two other centers, Coastal Hazards and Visual and Data Analytics, have also conducted research in support of the Coast Guard. Given the scope of our audit, we did not interview officials with these centers.

[14]Annual progress reviews may result in several outcomes, from no changes to a center to corrective actions or reduction in funding. The Office of University Programs also conducts a formal midterm review with subject matter experts to decide, among other things, which research areas will be continued. A cooperative agreement is a legally binding agreement that establishes terms and conditions (such as what work will be completed and when), as well as roles and responsibilities.

[15]When the Homeland Security Act of 2002 transferred the Coast Guard to the newly established DHS, it provided that the Coast Guard is to be maintained as a distinct entity within the department and that the authorities, functions, and capabilities of the Coast Guard to perform its missions are to be maintained intact. Pub. L. No. 107-296, § 888, 116 Stat. 2135, 2249 (codified at 6 U.S.C. § 468).

[16]The Coast Guard's 11 major missions are (1) ports, waterways, and coastal security; (2) drug interdiction; (3) aids to navigation; (4) search and rescue; (5) living marine resources; (6) marine safety; (7) defense readiness; (8) migrant interdiction; (9) marine environmental protection; (10) ice operations; and (11) other law enforcement.

DNDO

The Transformational & Applied Research Directorate seeks to develop technologies that will have a dramatic impact on capabilities to detect nuclear threats. The Transformational & Applied Research Directorate consists of staff focusing in these areas: Exploratory Research Program (ERP), Small Business Innovative Research (SBIR), Academic Research Initiative (ARI), and Advanced Technology Demonstration (ATD).

Below: handheld radiation detectors.

Source: GAO.

specific pieces of technology or prototypes. Its end users are typically other units within the Coast Guard, such as its Office of Boat Forces or Deployable Specialized Forces.

DNDO also conducts R&D applicable to border and maritime security, as it relates to its mission of detecting the use of an unauthorized nuclear explosive device, fissile material, or radiological material in the United States.[17] After its establishment, in 2005, DNDO assumed responsibility from S&T for certain nuclear and radiological R&D activities, and its R&D efforts are primarily conducted and managed by its Transformational and Applied Research Directorate (TARD).[18] DNDO's R&D efforts result in technology prototypes, development of software, and computer modeling for the detection of radioactive and nuclear materials. These efforts are crosscutting, meaning they can be used in more than just a border and maritime environment.

Each of DHS's border and maritime R&D organizations uses a different process to determine which R&D projects to pursue. S&T BMD reaches out to DHS-level officials as well as with operational-level end users, such as Border Patrol agents, to discuss needs, resources, and priorities and to determine which projects to initiate and also which projects should be continued or discontinued. BMD officials said that depending upon whom they speak with—that is, headquarters-level officials versus field-level operators—they often receive different answers regarding needs and priorities. Further, it is the role of the S&T project manager to facilitate agreement and consensus among the different offices within the component. The Coast Guard seeks input from its internal offices and its long-term strategies to identify capability gaps or ideas for new technological solutions, which are then evaluated based on available funding and other priorities into a prioritized ranking of projects that can be typically executed within 2 fiscal years. Some projects require more than 2 years. DNDO officials stated that their process for selecting and prioritizing projects is based on a review of capability gaps and

---

[17]DNDO was established by National Security Presidential Directive 43, Homeland Security Presidential Directive 14, and the Security and Accountability for Every Port Act of 2006 (SAFE Port Act). Pub. L. No. 109-347, § 501(a), 120 Stat. 1884, 1932 (codified at 6 U.S.C. §§ 591-596).

[18]See 6 U.S.C. § 592 (codifying the DNDO mission as including a number of R&D activities, including conducting an "aggressive, expedited, evolutionary, and transformational program of research and development").

government priorities in accordance with the Global Nuclear Detection Architecture as well as the Nuclear Defense R&D Road Map fiscal years 2013 to 2017. DNDO officials also stated that they consider what technologies exist before considering advanced technology development and their goal is to complete an R&D project with a proof-of-concept study or a prototype.

DHS's Border and Maritime R&D Budget and Projects

The S&T Directorate, DNDO, and the Coast Guard are each appropriated funding for R&D. Table 1 provides DHS's R&D budgets from fiscal years 2010 through 2013 for the various entities that conduct border and maritime R&D. A portion of each component's budget is dedicated to border and maritime R&D. However, as we reported in September 2012, DHS did not know how much its components invest in R&D, making it difficult to oversee R&D efforts across the department. For example, we reported that data DHS submitted to OMB showed that DHS's R&D budget authority and outlays were underreported because DNDO did not properly report its R&D budget authority and outlays to OMB for fiscal years 2010 through 2013. Specifically, for fiscal years 2010 through 2013, DHS underreported its total R&D budget authority by at least $293 million and outlays for R&D by at least $282 million because DNDO did not accurately report the data.[19] We also identified an additional $255 million in R&D obligations for fiscal year 2011 by other DHS components. Further, we found that DNDO did not report certain R&D budget data to OMB, and R&D budget accounts include a mix of R&D and non-R&D spending, further complicating DHS's ability to identify its total investment in R&D.

[19]GAO-12-837

GAO-13-732 DHS Border and Maritime R&D

Table 1: R&D Budgets for DHS for Science and Technology Directorate, the Coast Guard, and the Domestic Nuclear Detection Office, Fiscal Years 2010-2013

Dollars in millions

Component/office	2010 (enacted)	2011 (enacted)	2012 (enacted)	2013 (enacted)
S&T Research and Development, Acquisitions and Operations[a]	$856	$626	$533	$674
Coast Guard Research and Development	$24.7	$24.7	$27.8	$19.6
DNDO Transformational Research and Development	$109	$96	$40	$74.7

Source: DHS.

[a] This includes S&T's five divisions, University Programs, and Laboratory Facilities

As of June 2013, DHS had 95 ongoing R&D projects related to border and maritime security. See table 2 below for the number and total anticipated cost of ongoing border and maritime R&D projects by performing office.

Table 2: Current DHS Border and Maritime Projects by Component

Performing office	Number of current projects	Total anticipated project costs from start to end (Dollars in millions)[a]
S&T Borders and Maritime Security Division	11	$178.4
S&T University Programs[b]	34	$23.2
Coast Guard[c]	22	$53
Domestic Nuclear Detection Office	28	$70.5
Total	**95**	**$325.1**

Source: DHS.

[a] These amounts represent DHS's estimates of total project costs, including funding expended as well projected costs for fiscal years 2014- 2018. According to GAO's prior work, these amounts may be understated as they may not capture additionally contracted work. These projects are ongoing as of fiscal year 2013.

[b] This represents all border and maritime R&D across seven Centers of Excellence.

[c] Coast Guard homeland security projects—each project in the Coast Guard's Research Development Test and Evaluation Program portfolio is funded with a Research Development Test and Evaluation, Acquisitions, Construction & Improvement, or Operating Expenses appropriation.

It is important to note the total amount of resources and spending dedicated to R&D projects, and the final result and impact of these projects can vary dramatically based on the scope and purpose of the project. Some R&D projects aim to produce a specific prototype or piece of technology for an end user, such as sensors that CBP can use to better detect tunnels, nonlethal weapons Coast Guard can use to disable a boat's outboard engines, or a range of contraband marker systems.

GAO-13-732 DHS Border and Maritime R&D

Other projects may produce software to integrate information technology systems, such as software to integrate and display information gathered by multiple sensor systems. Finally, other projects may produce a report or knowledge product, which aims to inform an acquisition decision, such as providing the preliminary research required for developing a statement of work—a key step in the acquisition process. Individual R&D projects can range in cost from several thousand dollars to millions per fiscal year.

R&D Results Include Knowledge Products, Technology Prototypes, and Software, but S&T Should Do More to Obtain Feedback and Evaluate the Impact of Its Efforts

Costs and Types of Completed Border and Maritime R&D Projects Varied

Between fiscal years 2010 and 2012, DHS border and maritime R&D agencies reported producing 97 deliverables at an estimated cost of about $177 million and 29 discontinued projects at a cost of about $48 million.[20] An R&D deliverable can yield a variety of results. For example, an R&D deliverable, such as a report or a prototype, can be provided to a customer and then transitioned into an acquisition program or further developed by that customer; delivered, but not used for various reasons, or discontinued prior to delivery.[21]

---

[20] These amounts are a portion of the costs and are likely understated, as BMD was unable to provide GAO with cost information of specific transitions because of shared costs, and specific projects costs were not available for all Centers of Excellence by project.

[21] S&T defines a transition as a project output that is provided to a customer (such as CBP) that it puts into operational use and for which it assumes all of the operation and maintenance costs. All other project outputs provided to customers are called deliverables.

Twenty-nine projects were discontinued prior to their delivery to a customer. There were a variety of reasons that projects were discontinued, and it is important to note that the discontinuation of a project or deliverable did not necessarily mean that it was a failed R&D project. In some cases, the R&D results demonstrated that there was no technologically feasible option to address a problem or that a certain type of technology would not provide the desired solution. For example, DHS's Office of University program officials stated that they expect to routinely discontinue projects that are not demonstrably innovative, progressing, or have no identifiable end user, and reallocate resources to new innovative projects or to projects with specified customer interest. Further, according to the officials, project discontinuation is a good outcome in many circumstances where research success cannot be foretold. These officials added that it is a necessary part of a portfolio-based research strategy. Office of University program R&D and discontinued research projects are discussed in more detail later in this report.

Projects are also discontinued or merged into other projects because of a lack of available data, budget cuts, or DHS management determining that a project was no longer a priority to its potential customers. For example, S&T BMD officials stated insufficient funding resulted in the discontinuation of 2 projects, and for 2 other projects, the customer's priorities shifted and the R&D was terminated. In addition, DNDO stated that it determined that some methods for detection of shielded nuclear material were feasible but too costly and that certain detection devices would be too large for practical use in the field, so the R&D was discontinued. Table 3 provides the costs of R&D projects with deliverables, including discontinued projects, for fiscal years 2010 through 2012. See appendix I for a list of all the R&D projects and their deliverables for fiscal years 2010 through 2012 by component or office, project type, and their associated costs.

Table 3: Number of R&D Deliverables Reported for Fiscal Years 2010 through 2012

R&D performer	Number of deliverables provided to a customer	Total amount expended (Dollars in millions)		Number of projects or deliverables that were discontinued	Total amount expended for discontinued R&D (Dollars in millions)[a]
S&T Borders and Maritime Security Division	20	28.7		4[b]	33.0
S&T Office of University Programs– Centers of Excellence	18	6.1		19	Unknown
US Coast Guard	23	26.4		0	Not applicable
Domestic Nuclear Detection Office	36	$115.9		6	$15.4
Total delivered deliverables	**97**	**$177.1**	**Total discontinued projects**	**29**	**$48.4**
Total deliverables or projects (delivered and discontinued)	126				
Total expended (delivered and discontinued)(in millions)		$225.5			

Source: DHS data.

[a]These amounts are a portion of the costs and are likely understated, as BMD was unable to provide GAO with the costs of development of specific deliverables because of shared costs, and specific projects costs were not available for all Centers of Excellence projects by individual project due to the nature of grant funding reporting.

[b] Each DHS S&T BMD project can have multiple deliverables. The S&T BMD number represents projects, not deliverables.

DHS R&D deliverables were wide-ranging in their cost, scope, and scale. For example, agencies reported producing deliverables ranging from the development of imaging and radar prototypes to container screening devices and written market analyses of commercially available technologies. These 97 deliverables fell into three general categories: (1) knowledge products or reports; (2) technology prototypes; and (3) software, as listed in table 4.

GAO-13-732 DHS Border and Maritime R&D

Table 4: Type of Project Deliverable Provided to Customers, as Reported by R&D Performer

R&D performer	Knowledge product or report	Technology prototype	Software	Total
S&T Borders and Maritime Security Division	5	11	4	**20**
S&T Centers of Excellence	9	1	8	**18**
US Coast Guard	21	1	1	**23**
Domestic Nuclear Detection Office	3	15	18	**36**
Total	**38**	**28**	**31**	**97**

Source: DHS.

Knowledge products or reports: Thirty-eight of the 97 deliverables (39 percent) resulted in knowledge products that contained analysis and comparison testing of technologies, summarized field testing of technologies, or developed reference materials for use by DHS components. For example, one of the DHS Centers of Excellence developed formulas and models to assist in randomizing Coast Guard patrol routes and connecting networks together to assist in the detection of small vessels. Additionally, the Coast Guard conducted a technology evaluation to help its acquisition office determine the best tactical radios for use by law enforcement boarding teams.

Technology prototypes: Twenty-eight of the 97 deliverables (29 percent) resulted in technology prototypes, such as the development of new sensors, imaging equipment, or devices for detecting nuclear material. For example, S&T BMD developed prototype radar and upgraded video systems for use by Border Patrol agents and a prototype scanner to screen interior areas of small aircraft without removing panels or the aircraft skin. See figure 1 for an example of a prototype product developed by BMD for CBP.

Source. DHS.

Software: Thirty-one of the 97 deliverables (32 percent) resulted in the development of software, such as algorithms used in detection systems. For example, BMD developed software that enables intelligence personnel to quickly survey large areas of ocean and find vessels of interest. Additionally, DNDO developed software that extracts data from radiation portal monitors and uses the data to improve algorithms used in detecting radioactive material.

Customers Reported Mixed Views on the Impact of DHS's Border and Maritime R&D Project Deliverables

S&T BMD, the Coast Guard, and DNDO's R&D customers had mixed views regarding the impact of the R&D products or deliverables they received. Of the 126 R&D deliverables or projects DHS completed or discontinued from fiscal years 2010 through 2012, we interviewed DHS-identified customers or other relevant officials for 33 of these (19 customers and 6 program managers of 20 S&T BMD deliverables, 8 Coast Guard customers or other relevant officials of 8 deliverables or completed projects, and 2 DNDO project managers of 5 projects. Given our scope, we discussed ongoing and completed projects managed by S&T's Office of University Programs with Coast Guard and CBP, but did not systematically follow up with the recipients of each deliverable produced by the border and maritime related Centers of Excellence.

S&T BMD

Of the 20 S&T BMD deliverables, the customers of 7 deliverables stated that the deliverables met their office's needs, customers of 7 did not, and customers of 4 did not know, and customers for 2 could not be identified, as detailed below in table 5. For example, customers within CBP's Office of Technology Innovation and Acquisition reported that BMD's analysis and test results on aircraft-based use of wide area surveillance technology helped CBP to make a decision on whether it should pursue acquiring such technology. Another customer (DHS personnel assigned to the Joint Interagency Task Force South United States Southern Command) reported that software developed by BMD to enable analysts to quickly find and characterize small maritime vessels in an image showing large areas of ocean was highly valuable and met their office's needs.

Table 5: Science and Technology Directorate Borders and Maritime Security Division (S&T BMD) Fiscal Years 2010 through 2012 Deliverables and Customer Responses on Deliverable Usefulness

S&T BMD project deliverable	Customer identified by S&T BMD	Customer reporting on whether project deliverable met needs
Safe Quick Undercarriage Immobilization Device	CBP/Border Patrol	Unknown. S&T involvement ended prior to Customer involvement.
P25 Blue Force Tracking	CBP/Border Patrol, Office of Information Technology	Yes
Smart Integration Manager Ontologically Networked	CBP/Air and Marine Operations Center Coast Guard	No. Project is delayed. May meet needs in the future.
Sensor Management System	CBP/Office of Air and Marine	No. Project is delayed. May meet needs in the future.
Riverine Airboat	CBP/Office of Air and Marine	No. Prototype did not meet CBP needs.
Shipboard Automatic Identification System and Radar Contact Reporting System	CBP/Office of Air and Marine, Air and Marine Operations Center	Unknown. Customers identified by S&T were not familiar with project.
Maritime Asset Tag Tracking System	CBP/Office of Field Operations	No. Not used, pending results from another project.
Container Security Device	CBP/Office of Field Operations	No. Not used, pending results from another project.
Ground RADAR Comparison Testing	CBP/Office of Technology Innovation and Acquisition	Yes. Met customer needs and informed additional testing.

S&T BMD project deliverable	Customer identified by S&T BMD	Customer reporting on whether project deliverable met needs
Wide Area Airborne Sensor System	CBP/Office of Technology Innovation and Acquisition	Yes. Met customer needs and informed additional testing.
Wide Area Airborne Sensor Fixed Wing Testing	CBP/Office of Technology Innovation and Acquisition	Yes. Met customer needs and informed additional testing.
Wide Area Motion Imagery	Unknown	Unknown. S&T and CBP were unable to identify a customer.
Aviation Scanner	CBP/Office of Field Operations	No. CBP determined technology was not needed, but additional testing is planned to identify other potential uses.
Tipsheet Review And Correlation EnhanceR	Joint Interagency Task Force South	Yes. Technology met customer needs.
Low Light Camera	Joint Interagency Task Force South	Yes. Technology met customer needs.
Container Security Test Bed	CBP	No. Unclear if it has been used by CBP or if it has met CBP needs. Has been used by vendors for testing.
VizTools	Coast Guard	Yes. Prototype used to inform enterprise wide system.
Tethered Aerostat Radar Adjunct Radar Processor System	Unknown	Unknown. Customer could not be identified by S&T and the Coast Guard. After prototype was destroyed in a storm, R&D was not continued.
Mobile Surveillance System Imager Upgrade	CBP/Office of Technology Innovation and Acquisition	Unknown. Testing is ongoing.
Carrizo Cane	CBP/Office of Border Patrol	Unknown. Project was transferred to US Department of Agriculture.

Source: GAO analysis of DHS and S&T BMD data.

Conversely, of 20 deliverables, customers of 7 deliverables reported that the deliverable did not meet their office's needs. In cases where customers said that the deliverables were not meeting their needs, the customers explained that budget changes, other ongoing testing efforts, or changes in mission priorities were the reasons deliverables had not met their needs, and customers pointed out that their relationship with S&T had been positive and highly collaborative. In other cases, customers pointed out that while the deliverable had not been used as intended, it informed their office's decision making and helped to rule out certain technologies as possibilities. In this regard, the customers felt the R&D was successful, despite the fact that the deliverable had not or was not being used. Further, customers of 4 deliverables did not know or could not determine if the deliverable met their office's needs, and customers for 2 deliverables could not be identified by S&T, CBP, or the Coast Guard. BMD officials described, for example, why some of these older projects did not have identifiable customers and also described actions it had taken to help ensure that new projects have clear, committed customers. Under S&T's former process for initiating projects—which was carried out under S&T's former Undersecretary and dissolved by its current Undersecretary—BMD officials said that the potential existed to engage in R&D without a clear commitment from a customer. In February 2012, S&T issued a new project management guide that requires project managers to specify the customer by office and name, and to describe customer support for the project, including how the customer has demonstrated commitment for and support of the project. BMD officials said they believed this new process would prevent future R&D funding from going towards projects without a clear customer.

Coast Guard

The Coast Guard reported producing 23 deliverables from fiscal year 2010 through fiscal year 2012, and we met with officials involved with 8 of those projects, as listed in table 6. For 4 of 8 deliverables, Coast Guard officials reported that the deliverables had met internal Coast Guard needs. For example, one customer reported using a Coast Guard report on secure tactical radio communications systems to jump-start market research and to help develop a statement of work in developing the acquisition documents for the new radios. The customer said that the Coast Guard report did a good job of defining requirements and summarizing the needs of the operational end users—in this case, Coast Guard boarding teams. Ultimately, the customer said 762 radios were acquired and end users reported the radios were a vast improvement over what they had possessed in the past. For 3 of 8 deliverables, the impact was unknown because the research was ongoing. Finally, for 1 of 8 deliverables, the customer was unknown or could not be determined. For example, for the Low-Cost Swimmer Detection System, DHS S&T was identified as the customer, but an S&T official we spoke with said that S&T was the project manager and the Coast Guard was actually the customer. Ultimately, the project did not continue due to changes in Coast Guard budget priorities.

Regarding the 15 Coast Guard deliverables we did not discuss with customers, many of these were identified by the Coast Guard as deliverables but were different in nature from the deliverables discussed with S&T's customers. Further, the nature of the customers was different, too, since in some cases the customer was the Coast Guard's own R&D Center in order to support maintaining the R&D Center's capabilities for conducting technological and analytical support. For instance, while many of S&T's deliverables were prototypes or demonstrations for customers outside of S&T, the Coast Guard's deliverables were used within the Coast Guard and included such things as the independent validation and verification of the Coast Guard's maritime security risk analysis model, analysis support, and the Deepwater Horizon spill response.

Table 6: Coast Guard Fiscal Years 2010 through 2012 Deliverables and Customer Responses on Deliverable Usefulness

Project name	Customer identified by Coast Guard	Customer reporting on whether project met needs
Automated Scene Understanding and Situational Awareness (Visualization Tools)[a]	S&T	Unknown, project is ongoing. Unknown if it has or will meet customer's needs. The Coast Guard identified this as a deliverable, but S&T said the Coast Guard was the recipient. Deliverable was used to inform other work, but is limited by budget priorities.
Systematic Analysis of Deepwater Horizon Spill Response Technology	Coast Guard Research and Development Center and Director of Acquisition Services	Yes, project met customer needs and additional research is ongoing.[b]
Office of Naval Research Ship Stopping by Propeller Entanglement	Coast Guard Office of Specialized Capabilities	Unknown, project is ongoing

Unknown if it has or will meet customer needs |
| Integration of Law Enforcement Databases into Coast Guard Biometric System | Coast Guard Research and Development Center | Unknown, project is ongoing:

Unknown if it has or will meet customer's needs. |
Secure Tactical Connectivity [a]	Coast Guard Deployable Operations Group	Yes, project deliverable met customer's needs.
Low Cost Swimmer Detection System [a]	Unknown	Unknown. DHS customer could not be identified. Project ended with funding priority changes.
Support for Coast Guard High Latitude Region Mission Analyses	Coast Guard Research and Development Center and Office of Performance Management & Assessment	Yes, customer is within the Coast Guard, and documents are meeting Coast Guard's needs.[b]
Polar Icebreaker Business Case Analysis	Coast Guard Research and Development Center and Acquisition Program Manager, Surface	Yes, customers are internal to the Coast Guard and congressional requesters, and documents are meeting the Coast Guard's needs.[b]

Source: GAO analysis of Coast Guard data.

[a]DHS S&T was the project sponsor and Coast Guard R&D Center was the project executor.

[b]Customer feedback was provided by the Coast Guard R&D Center.

DNDO

DNDO reported producing 42 deliverables—which encompassed 6 discontinued projects and 36 projects that were either transitioned to the next phase of DNDO R&D or were completed and ended from fiscal years 2010 through 2012. We met with officials involved with 5 of those projects, as listed in table 7. According to DNDO Transformational and Applied Research Directorate (TARD) officials, they consider a project completed when it results in either a prototype or a knowledge product for integration into an acquisition program. Specifically, 17 of 36 projects were part of another ongoing DNDO project or Small Business Innovative

Research project and 19 of 31 projects were commercialized or concluded. DNDO R&D is different from the R&D of S&T or the Coast Guard for many reasons. For one, a DNDO project may start at a very low technology readiness level, in other words at the basic research level, but may end up being merged into other similar efforts in order to achieve a higher project goal. In these cases, the R&D customers are DNDO project managers, rather than an external DHS customer, such as CBP. We discussed 5 DNDO R&D deliverables at various R&D phases with DNDO officials—4 of which were deliverables from ongoing or completed projects and 1 of which was a discontinued project, as shown below in table 7.

Table 7: Select Domestic Nuclear Detection Office (DNDO) Deliverables and Project Outcomes

Project name	Customer identified by DNDO	Customer reporting on project met needs
Contextually-Aware Expert-System for Automated Threat Assessment	DNDO Transformational and Applied Research Directorate	Unknown, project is ongoing. Technology transitioned to another project. The project was one of DNDO's first broad agency agreements geared toward the national laboratories. The project's goal was to design a large data repository and use it to develop software that could be accessed by CBP officials when reviewing a single piece of cargo to determine its possible contents in a rapid manner.
High Yield Pulsed Neutron Generator	DNDO Transformational and Applied Research Directorate and outside entities	Yes, project was completed and commercialized. Adelphi Technologies developed a product out of this project and won a 2012 R&D award. The product that was developed was sold to universities and national labs. DNDO officials consider this a great success.
Study of Fast Neutron Signatures and Measurement Techniques for SNM Detection	DNDO Transformational and Applied Research Directorate	Yes, project was completed. The study findings suggest that conventional thermal neutron detection approaches with moderation are the preferred method for detecting neutron emitting sources in cargo. Study informed DNDO's decision making process as it pursues alternatives to Helium-3 for neutron detector systems.
Advanced Technology Demonstration for Shielded Nuclear Alarm Resolution Program - Multimodal Automated Resolution, Location, and Identification of Nuclear Material	DNDO Transformational and Applied Research Directorate	Yes, project is ongoing. Technology transitioned to another ongoing project.
Mapping isotopic distributions in cargo (FINDER) to detect Shielded Special Nuclear Material (SNM) and its configuration.	DNDO Transformational and Applied Research Directorate	Yes, project was discontinued. Technology found not feasible. Lessons learned informed other R&D.

Source: GAO analysis of DNDO data.

Given the different nature of DNDO's R&D efforts, we discussed the outcomes of DNDO's completed deliverables with their project managers and senior DNDO officials. DNDO TARD officials stated that their primary customers are themselves and DNDO's Acquisitions Directorate. We also met with officials from the DNDO directorates responsible for taking early-stage R&D work and moving it toward later-stage development and acquisitions. These officials said that the early stage R&D at DNDO feeds into the prioritized ranking of gaps in the global nuclear detection architecture[22], as well as into the analysis-of-alternatives phase of DNDO's solutions development process. Two of the 5 projects we discussed had moved from early-stage R&D into other projects further along in DNDO's project management process. Two of the 5 projects were completed, with 1 project providing information that informed DNDO decision-making processes, and the other project resulting in a commercialized product. Last, with regard to the 1 discontinued project, DNDO officials said there were many lessons learned, but that the particular project's technology was determined to be too expensive to continue pursuing.

Feedback Processes and Evaluation

Both the Coast Guard and DNDO reported having processes in place for gathering the views of customers regarding the results of R&D deliverables. For example, the Coast Guard RDT&E Program has a process in place for surveying its customers following the completion of a project and reported using this information for future R&D planning. The Coast Guard's survey instrument seeks feedback on the following items: customer satisfaction, timeliness, utility, and communications, among other things. The feedback step is part of the Coast Guard's Continuous Project Process. We reviewed 5 completed surveys from Coast Guard customers. The feedback included specific suggestions for improvements in the R&D process and positive comments regarding meeting customer needs and communication.

DNDO officials identified several ways in which they seek feedback from customers on the usefulness of their deliverables. For instance, in its solutions development process guide, DNDO provides direction to project managers on engaging in initial, small-quantity production of a system so

---

[22] The global nuclear detection architecture is an integrated system of radiation detection equipment and interdiction activities to combat nuclear smuggling in foreign countries, at the U.S. border, and inside the United States.

that the customer can thoroughly test the system in order to gain a reasonable degree of confidence as to whether the system actually performs to the agreed upon requirements before contracts for mass production are signed. For example, during the development of the Multimodal Automated Resolution, Location, and Identification of Nuclear Material project, DNDO managers reported gaining feedback from CBP officials through their participation in the R&D, since it is CBP who will be the eventual end user of the technology.[23] DNDO also details in its solutions development process guide how it works with customers to test fielded technology solutions, including documenting lessons learned and obtaining feedback as part of its R&D continuous development process. DNDO's internal R&D customers (other directorates) stated that they provided feedback on DNDO's R&D efforts through other mechanisms such as letters prioritizing technology needs and gaps. Coast Guard and DNDO officials also stated that it is not difficult to obtain feedback from their R&D customers, since their customers are generally within their own organizations.

Though S&T Borders and Maritime Security project managers seek feedback during their project execution, BMD does not gather and evaluate feedback from its customers to determine the impact of its completed R&D efforts and deliverables, making it difficult to determine if the R&D is meeting customer needs. Further, in some cases, the customer of S&T's R&D was not clear. For example, on BMD's Wide Area Motion Imagery project, BMD officials said that CBP was the customer of this deliverable, but CBP officials we spoke with did not know who was using the results of the R&D. However, on a project level, BMD officials stated that their office prepared reports related to this project and was told that the reports were helpful in CBP's broader consideration of options for new airborne sensor systems. In another S&T project, a Coast Guard customer identified by BMD was involved in testing the technology (the Tethered Aerostat Radio Processor) for BMD, but was not involved in the request for the R&D or in a position to make a determination on the extent to which the project met the Coast Guard's needs. Similarly, a CBP customer identified by BMD was aware of two R&D deliverables that BMD

---

[23]Multimodal Automated Resolution, Location and Identification of Nuclear Material (MARLIN)—the project seeks to optimize and characterize the ability of emerging technology to clear benign vehicles and containerized cargo of nuclear and radiological threats regardless of the shielding level in primary mode—the project costs approximately $17.5 million.

said were transitioned to his office, but the official was unable to provide additional information on the project's impact.[24] As we mentioned above, S&T recently made policy changes that require project managers to specify a project's customer by office and name and to describe customer support for the project at a project's outset. This change should help assist S&T in seeking feedback from its customers upon completion of a project.

For five projects, S&T BMD project managers and customers we met with could not provide definitive information on whether the deliverables had achieved their intended goals. For example, S&T and CBP officials agreed that R&D efforts on the Aviation Scanner project—a prototype scanner to screen interior areas of small aircraft without removing panels of the aircraft skin; however, the impact on CBP's mission needs or its future acquisitions is unknown pending future demonstration and testing in 2013. The National Academy of Sciences have stated that evaluating the relevance and impact of R&D is a key stage of the R&D process and that measuring the impact of R&D activities requires looking to the end users and stakeholders for an evaluation of the impact of a research program, such as through polling or systematic outreach.[25]

According to S&T BMD officials, since they deal with multiple DHS components and are not within the same agencies as its customers, it is sometimes difficult to identify who the customer of the R&D is and also difficult to determine what the impact of the R&D was. S&T officials also stated that in S&T's 2012 update to its project management guide, in its project closeout process, S&T has included a step to collect feedback from all relevant customers and a template for collecting this feedback. However, the S&T officials stated that this has not yet been carried out and that much work remains to be done to ensure this outreach and feedback is collected. BMD officials agreed that a more rigorous feedback process would provide S&T leadership a better understanding of how S&T is serving its customers and public.

---

[24]The two projects were the Shipboard Automatic Identification System and Radar Contact Reporting System.

[25]National Academy of Sciences, *Best Practices in Assessment of Research and Development Organizations.*2012.

While S&T has developed a process and template to collect feedback at the end of each project and incorporated this into its project management plan, it does not plan to survey customers each time it provides a deliverable to the customer. As previously noted, S&T projects are often conducted over several years before they are concluded or in some cases merged into other projects. These projects also often produce multiple deliverables for a customer that meet a specific operational need. For example, the Ground Based Technologies project began in fiscal year 2006 and is slated to continue through fiscal year 2018. During this period, S&T has provided multiple R&D deliverables to CBP—including test results comparing different ground based radar systems, as previously mentioned. The National Academy of Sciences has stated that feedback from both R&D failures and successes may be communicated to stakeholders and used to modify future investments. Moreover, S&T has not established timeframes and milestones for when it will begin collecting and evaluating feedback on these projects nor stated if and when it plans to begin gathering feedback on deliverables, and incorporate it into its broader processes for setting R&D priorities and portfolios. According to A Guide to the Project Management Body of Knowledge, which provides standards for project managers, specific goals and objectives should be conceptualized, defined, and documented in the planning process, along with the appropriate steps, time frames, and milestones needed to achieve those results.[26] Establishing time frames and milestones for collecting and evaluating feedback from its customers could help S&T better determine the usefulness and impact of its R&D projects and deliverables and make better-informed decisions regarding future work.

---

[26]Project Management Institute Inc., *A Guide to the Project Management Body of Knowledge (PMBOK® Guide), Fifth Edition,* (Newton Square, PA: 2013). All rights reserved.

DHS Has Taken Steps to Coordinate Border and Maritime R&D, but Opportunities Exist to Further Strengthen Internal and External Coordination

DHS Uses Various Approaches to Internally Coordinate R&D; Broader Efforts to Develop Departmental Policies for Overseeing and Coordinating R&D Are Ongoing

S&T's BMD, the Coast Guard, and DNDO reported taking a range of actions to coordinate with one another and their customers to ensure that R&D is addressing high priority needs. Officials from BMD identified several ways in which it coordinates R&D activities with its customers, which are primarily offices within CBP.

- **Agency details and Integrated Product Teams**: BMD officials reported having a person detailed to CBP's Office of Technology Innovation and Acquisition and identified its integrated product teams, such as its cross border tunnel threat team, and jointly funded projects as ways in which the division works to ensure its R&D efforts are coordinated with CBP.[27]
- **Joint strategies**: To improve coordination with its customers, in 2012, S&T began developing joint R&D strategic plans with various CBP offices that are designed to help ensure projects are addressing the highest-priority needs. S&T officials developed a draft strategy with the Office of Border Patrol in June 2013 and are planning throughout the rest of 2013 to develop strategies with other CBP offices, as well as a strategy with the Coast Guard in early 2014. BMD officials said that CBP's Office of Technology Innovation and Acquisition—which aims to ensure CBP's technology efforts are integrated across CBP and assists in managing new technology acquisitions—will be a signatory participant on all of the strategies. BMD also plans to

---

[27]In the integrated product teams, S&T officials interface directly with technology end users regarding their capability gaps and efforts already taken to address them. The integrated product teams were a formal institution under S&T's previous Under Secretary, but were since disbanded and are now maintained informally only in select topic areas.

develop broader component-level plans in the future. Presently, BMD uses letters of intent and technology transition agreements to coordinate with customers on a project-by-project level. These agreements identify specific project objectives and are detailed to an individual project. [28]

Officials from the Coast Guard's R&D Center identified several ways in which it coordinates with its customers (which are typically other offices within the Coast Guard).

- **Annual project cycle**: Officials identified the Coast Guard's annual project cycle as one of its primary mechanisms for coordinating with its internal customers to ensure that R&D efforts are addressing the most pressing operational needs. The annual project cycle involves the selection and ranking of its R&D portfolio extending out 2 fiscal years. To develop this portfolio, the Coast Guard has both an annual idea submission process and annual workshops, where officials develop the R&D Center project portfolio.[29] Ideas for new projects can come from any rank or office, and R&D Center officials said that they will consider all the ideas they receive.
- **Technology transition agreements**: The Coast Guard RDT&E Program also uses internal technology transition agreements to ensure that internal Coast Guard customers and stakeholders are prepared to move forward with an R&D prototype product when delivered. These technology transition agreements are non-binding agreements, internal to the Coast Guard, for ensuring the coordination and transition of R&D products.
- **Technology summits**: In an effort to enhance awareness of R&D efforts across DHS, in February 2012, the Coast Guard hosted a joint science and technology summit wherein the Coast Guard, BMD, and S&T Office of University Programs officials gave overview briefs of their respective work. The summit discussion included such topics as the value of routine meetings between the Coast Guard's R&D

---

[28]A technology transfer agreement is a non-binding agreement between participants to pursue common objectives and execute programs toward mutually beneficial objectives. A technology transfer agreement describes the following: customer operational need, desired deliverable(s) to meet this need, high level technical requirements, project schedule and funding, transition approach, and integration strategy.

[29]The Coast Guard's annual workshops focus on defined gap areas, such as underwater security needs or cyber security. The workshops are attended by high ranking Coast Guard officials, DHS and Department of Defense officials, experts in the particular topic, and anyone else with a vested interest (such as recreational boating groups).

program and various S&T divisions, as well as the successes that S&T has had working with CBP and the potential for the Coast Guard to determine if it can identify and replicate successful ways to increase its interactions with S&T.

DNDO also has several mechanisms for coordinating its R&D efforts that vary depending upon the maturity of the technology. For technologies that are close to deployable, DNDO's Architecture and Plans Directorate, which does not conduct R&D, engages directly with CBP and other potential customers to identify what technology enhancements the components need and then formulates plans and recommendations for solutions. For example, DNDO officials testified in 2010 that DNDO had outfitted the Coast Guard with over 5,000 personal radiation detectors, and officials from the Architecture and Plans Directorate reported working closely with the Coast Guard to add a radiological nuclear module to the Coast Guard's terrorism risk model. DNDO's Transformational and Applied Research Directorate, which does conduct R&D, works with less mature technologies and therefore does not always interact directly with the operational components.

While BMD, the Coast Guard, and DNDO were each taking actions to coordinate with their R&D customers, work remains to be done at the departmental level to ensure border and maritime R&D efforts are mutually reinforcing and are being directed toward the highest priority needs.[30] We recently highlighted coordination of R&D efforts as a challenge for DHS and we made recommendations for improving coordination. We reported that S&T, which is statutorily required to coordinate R&D efforts across the department, has taken some steps to coordinate R&D efforts across DHS, but that the department's R&D efforts are fragmented and overlapping, which increases the risk of unnecessary duplication.[31] We recommended in September 2012 that DHS develop a description of the department's processes and roles and responsibilities for overseeing and coordinating R&D investments and efforts. As of June 2013, DHS had not made a decision about how it

---

[30]Collaboration can be broadly defined as any joint activity that is intended to produce more public value than could be produced when the organizations act alone. Further, we have reported that agencies can enhance and sustain their collaborative efforts by defining and articulating common outcomes, identifying and addressing needs by leveraging resources, and agreeing on roles and responsibilities.

[31] GAO-12-837.

specifically planned to address these recommendations. BMD officials reported in June 2013 that the directorate's efforts would likely begin at the project and office levels (specifically through the office level strategic plans S&T's Homeland Security Advanced Research Project Agency is developing with CBP and the Coast Guard), and from there, move to a departmental level. Until DHS has made broader determination about what policies and procedures will govern the roles and responsibilities for coordinating R&D, it will be unclear what the effectiveness of the various coordination approaches are.

Opportunities Exist for DHS to Enhance Coordination with Universities Conducting Research on Its Behalf

DHS S&T Office of University Programs officials discussed the variety of ways in which centers and DHS components collaborate and share information, and 4 of 5 center officials we met with were generally satisfied with the level of communication and collaboration between their centers and DHS. Projects at the centers have 5-year work plans that go through a mid-point review process with component-agency input where they can be reevaluated and modified. To solicit ideas for new projects, the Office of University Programs holds technical workshops with component-level subject matter experts. The component subject matter experts will discuss a technical or informational challenge they have, and as a group, the workshop participants will discuss what key research questions need to be addressed imminently. The Office of University Programs will draft these issues into more formalized research questions and put them out to the universities and centers. The office then examines proposals it receives based on how the research can further DHS's missions. Office of University Programs officials stated that the office's process for soliciting research topics and evaluating proposals is good and that it keeps the centers flexible. Center officials also reported collaborating on a variety of projects with non-DHS customers, such as DOD (specifically the Army Research Laboratory and the Air Force Office of Scientific Research), NOAA, the National Institute of Health, the National Science Foundation, and the Department of Justice.

However, officials from DHS's primary land border security Center of Excellence reported challenges with respect to a lack of clarity regarding protocols for access to DHS information when conducting R&D. Specifically, officials from this center reported that they have been regularly unable to obtain data from CBP to complete research it was conducting on CBP's behalf, which resulted in delays and terminated R&D projects. These officials reported that of 4 discontinued projects and 9 completed projects, 4 projects experienced delays, incomplete data, or incorrect data. Office of University Programs staff stated that misunderstandings surrounding procedures regarding nongovernmental personnel access to data can be a challenge.[32]

DHS Office of University Programs officials said in June 2013 that they have not fully developed all of the procedures regarding sharing government data. However, the officials said that under the terms of the cooperative agreements between the Office of University Programs and the centers, CBP has no obligation to provide government-generated data of any kind. The officials said that this is because universities generally operate under the principle of publishing at will, which could limit the ability of DHS to restrict the publication of potentially sensitive information. The Office of University Programs provides several avenues for DHS components to be involved with the centers and potential projects, including writing funding opportunity announcements for centers, selecting projects to fund, reviewing and negotiating work plans, and recommending corrections. But given the challenges raised by the primary border security center, the Office of University Programs could help ensure that the approximately $3 million to $4 million a year dedicated to each university center is used more effectively by more carefully considering data needs, potential access issues, and potential data limitations with its federal partners before approving projects. We have previously stated that identifying data sources and collection procedures is one of the five key steps to an effective evaluation design.[33] Further, we have stated that in selecting a product's design, agencies should determine a design's limitations as a result of the information required or the scope and methodology—such as questionable data quality or reliability, inability to access certain types of data, or security classifications or confidentiality restrictions—and to address how these limitations will affect the product. Given the challenges raised by officials from both universities leading the R&D for land border security, a more rigorous review of potential data-related challenges and limitations at the start of a project could help R&D customers (such as CBP) identify data requirements and potential limitations up front so that money is not allocated to projects that potentially cannot be completed. DHS Office of

---

[32]Under the terms and conditions of a cooperative agreement, university center researchers are prohibited from using or generating sensitive or classified information. However, centers operating under contracts managed directly by the component agencies, such as a Basic Ordering Agreement, could issue task orders to the centers of excellence that could include conditions allowing the sharing of sensitive information.

[33] GAO-12-208G.

University Programs officials agreed that making sure their clients take additional steps to identify data requirements up front could help address these challenges.

DHS Has Taken Steps to Coordinate with and Leverage R&D Efforts of Other Federal Agencies

DHS's R&D agencies reported regularly coordinating with the Department of Defense (DOD) and the Department of Energy (DOE) in the development of new border and maritime security technologies on both an individual project level and at a departmental level. For example, officials from S&T, the Coast Guard, and DNDO each reported having productive relationships with several DOD offices—including the Office of Naval Research; the Defense Threat Reduction Agency; the Army Night Vision Center; and the Army Research, Development, and Engineering Command. Specifically, DNDO officials said DNDO has an interagency agreement with DOD to develop long range nuclear detection devices. DNDO also has a memorandum of understanding with DOD's Defense Threat Reduction Agency, DOE's National Nuclear Security Administration, and the Office of the Director of National Intelligence to coordinate national nuclear detection R&D programs. Further, Coast Guard officials reported partnering with the Navy to develop unmanned aerial surveillance technologies capable of launching from the deck of a cutter and to develop systems to disable a boat's outboard engines, as shown in figure 2.

Figure 2: Vessel Entanglement System Developed by DOD and the Coast Guard

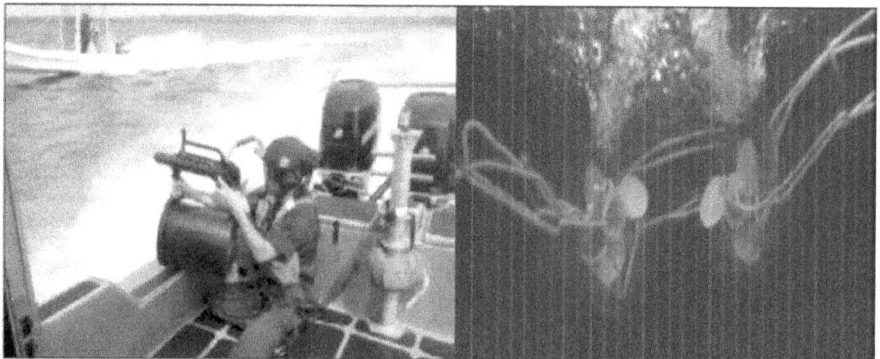

Source: USCG.

Additionally, Coast Guard, DNDO, and S&T have used the facilities at several of DOE's national laboratories, including the Pacific Northwest National Laboratory, the Savannah River National Laboratory, and the Lawrence Livermore National Laboratory. Within S&T, the Office of

National Laboratories is responsible for helping facilitate cooperative agreements between the national labs and DHS components and is to review all statements of work issued from DHS to the national laboratories. However, we reported in September 2012 that 11 DHS components had reimbursed the national laboratories for R&D between fiscal years 2010 and 2013, but the Office of National Laboratories could not provide us with any information on those activities and told us it did not track them.[34] Instead, the Office of National Laboratories told us it used other means to monitor DHS work at the laboratories such as relationships with components and S&T, reviewing task orders sent to the laboratories from DHS, visiting laboratories, and laboratories self-reporting their work.

Though it does not report conducting R&D, offices within CBP also reported coordinating directly with DOD offices—such the Joint Non-Lethal Weapons Program, Army Research, Development, and Engineering Command, and the Army's Acquisition, Technology, and Logistics Office—in the development and testing of particular technologies. For example, CBP's Office of Air and Marine reported visiting the Navy's laboratory facilities to learn more about the Navy's efforts to develop a device capable of disabling a boat's outboard engine through a directed energy source. The Navy was conducting this research in collaboration with the Coast Guard and the officials from the Office of Air and Marine asked to be kept apprised of the project's progress and to be allowed to participate in any testing and demonstrations of prototypes. DHS officials also reported participating with DOD on a variety of working groups, including the Air Domain Working Group and the Executive Aviation Commonality Working Group.

These collaborative relationships have had benefits for DOD as well. For instance, officials from the Office of Air and Marine reported working with the Navy when it was developing new ocean surveying software for tracking vessel movements. The Navy needed a specific number of testing hours on an air platform as well as sensor operators familiar with sea search radar systems before the software could move ahead in its development. The Office of Air and Marine and the Navy agreed, via a memorandum of agreement, to adapt the Navy's software to three

---

[34]We received obligations data for fiscal years 2010 and 2011, funding data for fiscal year 2012, and projected funding data for fiscal year 2013. GAO-12-837.

different types of Office of Air and Marine aircraft. The Navy funded the nonrecurring engineering and the Office of Air and Marine paid to install and integrate the software on its aircraft. Additionally, officials from CBP reported working with DOD to conduct joint testing on a vehicle immobilization device. The officials said that DOD had the funding to do the testing, but needed vehicles, which CBP had. CBP conducted the field testing of the devices and shared the data with DOD. In a 2011 testimony, a senior DOD official said that DOD and DHS were cosponsoring a tunnel detection capability demonstration and that technologies resulting from these efforts were expected to be fielded domestically and abroad.

Despite successes in the development of new security technologies, DHS and DOD have had fewer successes in the repurposing of already-existing DOD technologies for border and maritime security. CBP has an agreement with S&T to work with DOD on repurposing its technologies, such as laser scopes, radios, and surveillance equipment and DHS and DOD have tested some of these technologies in south Texas, but have identified several challenges with using the equipment. For example, the laser scopes used by DOD do not meet the eye safety requirements in place for federal law enforcement officers operating within U.S. borders. Second, radios that are developed by DOD for use in foreign countries do not always meet Federal Communications Commission requirements for use in the United States and cannot be easily reprogrammed. Additionally, use of certain surveillance aircraft used by DOD overseas is restricted in U.S. airspace and such aircraft therefore cannot be used by CBP. Officials from CBP's Office of Field Operations said that they were offered equipment from DOD, but were unable to acquire it because it did not meet specific CBP security requirements and was not compatible with CBP's existing operations and maintenance contracts. Specifically, Office of Field Operations officials said their office cannot service DOD's equipment with its existing vendor service contracts, and that operations and maintenance is a major factor in whether CBP can add something new to its fleet. For instance, officials from the Office of Field Operations said their office was offered DOD small X-ray vans. The office sent officials to inspect the vans and they concluded it would have required a substantial investment on CBP's part to get the vans into working condition and to upgrade them so that they could be integrated into CBP's existing fleet. DHS and DOD officials indicated that they would continue to work closely together to evaluate opportunities for integrating DOD equipment into DHS's homeland security efforts.

DHS Uses Workshops and Other Means to Coordinate Efforts with the Private Sector, but Most Coordination Takes Place on a Project Level

S&T, the Coast Guard, and DNDO coordinate with the private sector on a project level, as well as through conferences, industry days, and workshops. S&T refers to its external coordination efforts as technology foraging and it identified several ways in which it coordinates its border and maritime R&D efforts with the private sector. The six BMD program managers we spoke with—who were responsible for managing projects resulting in 18 R&D deliverables and 3 of BMD's current portfolios—said that at the start of every new project, they canvass industry experts to gather information on the current state of the art technologies, to gain expertise, and to identify where DHS's R&D efforts would be most beneficial. For example, as part of its project to research technologies to detect cross-border underground tunnels, BMD reached out to officials in the mining and oil industries to discuss their respective areas of expertise in using underground sensor systems. From this, BMD determined that the currently available technologies were not ideal for the type of detection capabilities DHS needed and used this information in developing a more effective sensor system for DHS.

The Coast Guard also identified several avenues through which it coordinates with the private sector. For instance, the Coast Guard's RDT&E Program uses broad agency announcements to survey industry to learn what technologies are already available. The Coast Guard also uses cooperative research and development agreements under the Technology Transfer Act to partner with industry on R&D projects and in July 2013 reported having six such agreements underway. Further, since 2000, the Coast Guard RDT&E Program has participated in the Coast Guard Innovation Exposition, which has assisted in informing Coast Guard decision makers about research that is completed, underway, or planned. The Innovation Exposition was designed to provide a forum to exchange ideas and collaborate within the Coast Guard and with its government, industry, and academic partners. Because of budget constraints, the Coast Guard suspended the exposition beyond 2011 and has stated that it is reevaluating the goals and outcomes of the expositions in terms of their cost and benefits.

DNDO reported engaging in similar forms of private industry outreach. For instance, DNDO hosts an annual industry day that is attended by officials from industry, academia, national laboratories, and others. As part of the industry day, DNDO reported collaborating with the private sector to discuss ways to enhance existing radiation detection devices and develop new technologies that will meet the needs of federal, state, and local law enforcement officials through programs such as the Commercial First initiative and the Graduated Radiation and Nuclear

Detector Evaluation and Reporting program. DNDO officials reported signing an industry engagement policy in April 2013 which stated how DNDO plans to meet directly with vendors to learn about new technologies. The policy provides guidance and a standard operating procedure for DNDO employees on holding structured meetings with vendors and exchanging information when researching commercially available technologies. It also identifies fundamental procurement principles, and provides guidance for meeting with vendors and industry representatives.

Beyond its project-level outreach, DHS S&T officials identified what they refer to as technology foraging as the directorate's approach for identifying and adapting already-available technologies in the private sector. In a draft June 2013 document, S&T stated that technology foraging is a formal and structured method for identifying technologies and research and that project managers should use this knowledge to, in part, conduct more informed project planning. To help integrate technology foraging into its regular project management, S&T established a Technology Foraging Office within its Research and Development Partnerships Group. S&T officials reported that staff from this office is available to provide technology foraging services to S&T project managers upon request. For example, in July 2013, S&T reported leveraging a coastal-weather radar system at the National Oceanic and Atmospheric Administration (NOAA) to supplement software S&T developed that lets the Coast Guard sweep a bay with radar as a way to track small anonymous boats or other vessels that transport drugs or other illegal contraband. Further, S&T invested $11 million in a private, not-for-profit strategic investment firm designed to coordinate advances in commercial technologies with the needs of the U.S. intelligence and security communities. S&T officials reported that this investment was designed to support technology foraging efforts. [35]

Conclusions

Securing the nation's land borders and waterways is a complicated undertaking requiring many elements, including effective and coordinated

---

[35]In addition to its technology foraging and investments, officials from BMD presented at numerous international conferences in 2012, including an April 2012 US-Canada border security summit; a May 2012 North Atlantic Treaty Organization symposium on port and regional maritime security in Lerici, Italy; and a June 2012 workshop on innovation in border control in Copenhagen, Denmark.

R&D programs. Border and maritime R&D efforts at DHS in recent years have resulted in dozens of deliverables to various DHS components. But these products have had varying levels of impact on DHS's ability to acquire new security technologies or to advance its homeland security missions. Establishing timeframes and milestones for collecting and evaluating feedback from its customers on the usefulness and impact of the R&D projects and deliverables they receive could help S&T ensure that the technologies being developed and delivered to the Coast Guard, Customs and Border Protection, U.S. Immigration and Customs Enforcement, and other DHS components are meeting customer needs and achieving their intended goals. Further, DHS has made progress leveraging the expertise and resources of academia through its Centers of Excellence, but has faced cancelled and delayed projects in some areas because of a lack of data from DHS. By ensuring that potential challenges and limitations with regard to data quality, accessibility, and availability are reviewed and understood prior to approving projects, DHS can help ensure that it focuses its resources on those projects that are better positioned for success.

Recommendations for Executive Action

To help ensure that DHS effectively manages and coordinates its border and maritime R&D efforts, we recommend that the Secretary of Homeland Security instruct the Under Secretary for Science and Technology to:

- establish timeframes and milestones for collecting and evaluating feedback from its customers to determine the usefulness and impact of its R&D projects and deliverables, and use it to make better-informed decisions regarding future work, and
- ensure that design limitations with regard to data reliability, accessibility, and availability are reviewed and understood before approving Center of Excellence R&D projects.

Agency Comments and Our Evaluation

We provided a draft of this report to DHS for its review and comment. DHS provided written comments, which are reproduced in full in appendix II, and concurred with our recommendations. DHS also described actions it plans to take to address the recommendations. Specifically, according to DHS, all DHS S&T project plans will be modified to require formalized feedback from its R&D customers at key project milestones, such as testing or transition of a deliverable. Further, to improve its consideration of potential data needs, access issues, and data limitations, DHS S&T plans to develop standard guidelines and protocols for all centers of excellence, which would describe, for example, how data sets must be modified to enable use in open-source, unrestricted research formats. DHS S&T also plans to encourage centers to voluntarily convene workshops to engage both researchers and DHS components to better understand constraints and to develop protocols for acquiring and using government data. DHS plans to complete these efforts by September 30, 2014. Such actions should address the overall intent of our recommendations.

DHS also provided written technical comments, which we incorporated as appropriate.

We are sending copies of this report to the Secretary of Homeland Security, appropriate congressional committees, and other interested parties. This report is also available at no charge on GAO's website at http://www.gao.gov.

If you or your staff have any questions about this report, please contact me at (202) 512-9627 or maurerd@gao.gov. Contact points for our Office of Congressional Relations and Public Affairs may be found on the last page of this report. Key contributors to this report are listed in appendix III.

David C. Maurer
Director,
Homeland Security and Justice Issues

Appendix I: Department of Homeland Security (DHS)
Border and Maritime List of Completed and
Discontinued Research and Development (R&D)
Project Deliverables for Fiscal Years 2010 through 2012

Table 8: List of United States Coast Guard – Homeland Security R&D Project Deliverables for Fiscal Years 2010 through 2012

United States Coast Guard (Coast Guard) - Homeland Security Related Projects

	Project name	Project description	Product type[a]	Total Project Cost[b]
1	Maritime Mass Rescue Interventions	Study of available interventions (methods and tools) for use by rescuers or good Samaritans in maritime mass rescue incidents.	Report	$135,500
2	Automatic Identification System in Maritime Aids to Navigation Analysis	The Coast Guard seeks a more economical and efficient solution for active aids to navigation than the current radar beacons.	Report	$167,173
3	Automated Scene Understanding and Situational Awareness[c]	The command center watchstander is burdened with increasing quantities of maritime domain sensors and situational information.	Letter, Brief, Report	$5,712,916
4	Deepwater Horizon Response	The federal on scene commander requires investigation of various concepts/technologies to support spill response efforts with respect to the Deepwater Horizon oil spill.	Report	$33,784
5	Systematic Analysis of Deepwater Horizon Spill Response Technology	The Coast Guard seeks to improve understanding of how technologies worked in Deepwater Horizon and what opportunities for improvement should be pursued.	Report	$263,309
6	Office of Naval Research Ship Stopping by Propeller Entanglement	The Coast Guard, DHS and Department of Defense (DOD) seek to improve capability to non-lethally stop a non compliant large vessel.	Report	$75,779
7	Test and Evaluation for Weapons of Mass Destruction (WMD) Response Pilot Program	The Coast Guard seeks to evaluate function of first responders in pre-selected new WMD personal protective equipment.	Prototype Equipment and report	$5,502,743
8	Integration of Law Enforcement Databases into Coast Guard Biometric System	The Coast Guard law enforcement and intelligence communities lack single point of entry access to federal databases to support search and enroll during at sea biometrics.	Brief	$810,195
9	Biometric Sector San Juan Helpdesk Support	Fast-paced proof of concept requires operational support to ensure the proper operation of prototype systems, adequate training, train the trainer, and collection of operational metrics.	Transition plan: pilot plan including concept of operations, instruction plan and quick reference guide	$1,567,716
10	Secure Tactical Connectivity[c]	Coast Guard boarding teams seek to improve reliability of voice and data communications between boarded vessels and support commands.	Technology capabilities and alternative analysis, test and evaluation results	$991,095
11	Non-Pyrotechnic Flashbang Grenade	Coast Guard tactical teams lack a diversionary device with the effects of conventional flashbangs without incurring secondary threats from excessive smoke or possible fire.	Market survey report, requirements definition report, and feasibility report	$355,958

Appendix I: Department of Homeland Security
(DHS) Border and Maritime List of Completed
and Discontinued Research and Development
(R&D) Project Deliverables for Fiscal Years
2010 through 2012

12	Hidden Compartment Contraband Detection	The Coast Guard seeks to improve current capabilities to detect contraband in hidden compartments.	Report	$217,916
13	Low Cost Swimmer Detection System[c]	The Coast Guard seeks low-cost underwater threat detection systems for protection of critical infrastructure.	Noned	$33,900
14	Barrier System Study Update	The information on current barrier technology countermeasures is not sufficient for decision making on their value in protecting High Value maritime assets from waterborne threats.	Report	$60,168
15	Support for Coast Guard High Latitude Region Mission Analyses	Coast Guard mission analysis reports guide future acquisition and mission development needs in the Arctic and Antarctic high latitude regions.	Analysis report	$2,300,502
16	Polar Icebreaker Business Case Analysis	No current summary of information is available to support decision makers with regards to the requirements, options, and cost of sustainment of the Coast Guard Polar icebreaking capability.	Independent report on a business case analysis, independent analysis, business case study, brief	$1,658,048
17	Ultra-High Frequency Operational Communications	The Coast Guard seeks to improve the ultra-high frequency radio communications capability introduced by the Rescue 21 system, affecting intra-Coast Guard communications as well as Coast Guard communications with other government agencies and port partners.	Brief and feasibility study	$375,564
18	Blue Force Tracking	The Coast Guard seeks to improve the ability to track/identify its own assets and people automatically during various mission conditions.	Report	$452,814
19	Fleet Mix Analysis–Phase 2	The Coast Guard seeks to develop fiscally constrained fleet mixes to support leadership decision making.	Case analysis	$840,461
20	USCG Sensor Operational Performance Data	The Coast Guard lacks sensor performance data needed as input to simulation models used to support acquisitions and future force mix decisions.	Prototype Software and report	$2,926.743
21	Maritime Security Risk Analysis Methodology Independent Verification and Validation (IV&V)	Understanding of how new explosive detection technologies and field operations can be effectively employed in the maritime environment	IV&V and accreditation plan, IV&V report	$366,761
22	Analysis Support for Coast Guard Unmanned Aerial System Implementation	Coast Guard seeks to improve its understanding of how land-based unmanned aerial system can be operated to support its missions.	Execution plan, procurement plan, & lessons learned Report	$981,916
23	Independent Analysis and Assessment of Fused Intel	The Coast Guard needs improved capability to effectively collect and correlate data and/or reduce data corruption from multiple inputs.	Independent assessment, field test and report	$571,905

Source: DHS.

[a]The Coast Guard provided the product type.

[b] Costs represent Total Project value, i.e., direct and government staff labor & overhead costs, and
may contain multiple years of funding and funding prior to fiscal year 2010. Each project in the Coast

Appendix I: Department of Homeland Security
(DHS) Border and Maritime List of Completed
and Discontinued Research and Development
(R&D) Project Deliverables for Fiscal Years
2010 through 2012

Guard's Research Development Test and Evaluation Program portfolio is funded with a Research Development Test and Evaluation, Acquisitions, Construction & Improvement, or Operating Expenses appropriation.

[c]DHS S&T was the project sponsor and Coast Guard R&D Center was the project executor.

[d]S&T informed us they were the project manager and this resulted in a comparison report

Table 9: Science and Technology Directorate (S&T) Borders and Maritime Security Division (BMD) Project Deliverables for Fiscal Years 2010 to 2012

Science and Technology Directorate (S&T) Borders and Maritime Security Division (BMD) Project Deliverables

	Project name	Project descriptions	Product type	Total project costs[a]
1	Safe Quick Undercarriage Immobilization Device (SQUID)	Prototype of a remotely operated mechanical vehicle stopping device.	Prototype	$850,000
2	P25 Based Blue Force Tracking	Asset tracking capability that employs existing P25 radio infrastructure.	Software	$250,000
3	Smart Integration Manager Ontologically Networked (SIMON)	SIMON is an integration platform for data-producing systems, and an integration process for streamlining the modernization and modularization of new and existing systems.	Software	$3,990,000
4	Sensor Management System (SMS)	A real-time sensor integration and distribution system. SMS is used to incorporate local and regional sensor data to help enhance track picture at command centers.	Prototype	Not Available
5	US Customs and Border Protection (CBP) Riverine Airboat Ballistic Protection	Prototype riverine airboat system that provides ballistic protection to operators.	Prototype	$376,000
6	Shipboard Automatic Identification System and Radar Contact Reporting System	Use participating maritime vessels as "additional eyes" to help detect and track other boats by exfiltrating vessel's on-board radar data and relaying received automatic identification system messages via satellite link to a ground node.	Prototype	$1,175,000
7	Maritime Asset Tag Tracking System	Provides communications of an unauthorized container door opening or tampering detection, along with tracking information, to a central data collection system.	Prototype	
8	Container Security Device	Provides warning of unauthorized container door opening or tampering.	Prototype	$5,800,000
9	Ground RADAR Comparison Testing	Provide CBP's Office of Technology Innovation and Acquisition (OTIA) with performance data and suitability information for commercial off-the the shelf (COTS) radars that could be used on towers or Mobile Surveillance Systems for border surveillance. To be utilized for requirements development and procurement specifications.	Report on field tests	$1,925,000
10	Wide Area Airborne Sensor System Testing	Report delivered to CBP and the Coast Guard on test and evaluation of the system in the Tucson Sector, to assist future acquisition assessment.	Report on field tests	$373,171

Science and Technology Directorate (S&T) Borders and Maritime Security Division (BMD) Project Deliverables

11	Wide Area Airborne Sensor System Testing	Report delivered to CBP and the Coast Guard on test and evaluation of the system in the Tucson Sector, to assist future acquisition assessment.	Report on field tests	$358,871
12	Wide Area Motion Imagery	Report delivered to CBP and the Coast Guard on test and evaluation of the system in the Tucson Sector, to assist future acquisition assessment.	Report	$183,393
13	Aviation Scanner	Prototype system to examine the interior areas of light aircraft without removing panels or aircraft skin/covers.	Prototype	$1,000,000
14	Tipsheet Review And Correlation EnhanceR	Software application that enables operators to quickly survey large areas of ocean and find vessels of interest.	Software	Not Available
15	Low-light Camera	Track low observable targets.	Prototype	Not Available
16	Container Security Test Bed	Technology to "sniff" maritime containers for materials of interest. The test bed is a spin-off being used by community for realistic testing of new cargo security technology.	Prototype	$3,400,000
17	Viz Tools	Defined business process and user interface requirements for future operational requirements document	Software	$2,676,000
18	Tethered Aerostat Radar Adjunct Radar Processor System	Provides for the detection, tracking and reporting on vessel activity in the Mona Passage (strait between Puerto Rico and Hispaniola).	Prototype	$800,000
19	Mobile Surveillance System (MSS) Imager/Radar Upgrade	Retrofit kit to enhance radar, imager, and graphical user interface/mapping for CBP's current MSS units.	Prototype	$2,500,000
20	Carrizo Cane	Research into the use of biological control agent to eliminate non-native weeds that create a security hazard along the southwest border. Included quarantine, rearing, and field deployment studies. The US Department of Agriculture is funding scale-up and deployment.	Report	$3,000,000

Source: DHS.

[a]Funding for projects may contain S&T and component funds.

Appendix I: Department of Homeland Security
(DHS) Border and Maritime List of Completed
and Discontinued Research and Development
(R&D) Project Deliverables for Fiscal Years
2010 through 2012

Table 10: Domestic Nuclear Detection Office (DNDO) R&D Project Deliverables for Fiscal Years 2010 to 2012

Domestic Nuclear Detection Office (DNDO) Projects

	Project name	Project description	Product type	Total project costs
1	Passive Detection of Shielded Special Nuclear Material (SNM)	Development of a system of algorithms, intermediate-scale neutron and gamma-ray counters, and performance metrics to passively identify the presence of SNM by neutron-induced nuclear fission reactions that create bursts of many neutrons and gamma rays.	Software-algorithms	$6,436,314
2	Integrating Portal Monitors with Individual Source Identification, Tracking	Development of a portal-less monitor, the Roadside Tracker integrating both video and gamma ray imagining technology.	Prototype	$6,732,483
3	Contextually-Aware Expert-System for Automated Threat Assessment	Combine gamma and neutron measurements with non-radiation and contextual information to vastly improve threat/non-threat discrimination and radiation alarm resolution through the use of training tables and machine learning.	Software-algorithms	$6,087,722
4	Physics and Algorithm Enhancements for a Validated MCNP/X Monte Carlo Simulation Tool	Develop and implement several key physics and algorithm enhancements in areas where the code was lacking, improvements in evaluated data and benchmark measurements for the MCNP/MCNPX Monte Carlo codes for active and passive detection systems.	Software-algorithms	$5,152,060
5	SoftWare for Optimization of Radiation Detectors	Development of an object-oriented and vertically-integrated radiation transport simulation and analysis system and provides an end-to-end environment for simulating gamma-ray background, nuisance sources, and targets of interest.	Software-algorithms	$4,493,957
6	Detection of Heavily Shielded Nuclear Contraband through Muon Radiography with Advanced Micro-pattern Detectors	Development of a muon radiography proof of concept prototype that utilizes a gas electron multiplier detector, promising shorter interrogation time and better spatial resolution compared with more traditional passive portal systems that detect dense objects such as special nuclear material.	Prototype	$748,671
7	Large Area X-ray Detector for Cargo Inspection	Development of a stacked array of cesium iodide panel detectors for significant improvement in detection capability for both contraband and special nuclear material at the required scan throughput.	Prototype	$2,694,293
8	Data Fusion for Nuclear Threat Detection	Production of receiver/operator characteristic curves and analytical determination of the amount of, and the reasons for, improvements of decisions based on fused data rather than simple Boolean combinations of decisions.	Study	$843,744

**Appendix I: Department of Homeland Security
(DHS) Border and Maritime List of Completed
and Discontinued Research and Development
(R&D) Project Deliverables for Fiscal Years
2010 through 2012**

Domestic Nuclear Detection Office (DNDO) Projects

	Project name	Project description	Product type	Total project costs
9	A Framework for Developing Novel Detection Systems Focused on Interdicting Shielded Helium Enriched Uranium (HEU)	Demonstrate the ability to develop and deploy new detector concepts with fully integrated signal and information analysis to attain breakthrough improvements in the nation's ability to detect domestic nuclear threats through the smuggled HEU interdiction through enhanced analysis and detection framework, which comprises four research teams (areas) covering: detectors, systems analysis, radiation transport and inversion, and a social science and policy.	Software-modeling	$4,959,000
10	Interdicting Smuggled Nuclear Material	Development of interdiction models, solution algorithms, insights and specific recommendations for optimally prioritizing sites for locating radiation detectors to thwart an intelligent and informed smuggler of nuclear material over a global transportation network, and to develop tools for rapid computation of physics-based detection probabilities that parametrically address a range of detectors, types of special nuclear material, and local conditions that in concert determine detection probabilities. .	Software-algorithms	$1,571,906
11	Multi-layered system level screening for port security	Explore how a systems approach can be used to design and analyze systems for detecting nuclear material at our nation's ports. The team developed a risk-based framework for screening cargo containers for nuclear material and developed an expert judgment tool to rank nuclear threat risk levels for incoming vessels.	Software-algorithms	$119,922
12	Stand-Off Radiation Detection System	Mobile passive detection systems with a goal of detection at a distance, 1mC at 100meters. The unit has a backplane made of cesium iodide logs and a passive mask/antimask on either side enabling dual sided coded aperture imaging.	Prototype	$5,466,047
13	Mobile Imaging and Spectroscopic Threat Identification	Mobile passive detection systems with a goal of detection at a distance, 1mC at 100m. The unit uses an array of high purity germanium (HPGe) detectors for high-resolution spectral triggering of the sodium iodide based coded aperture imager.	Prototype	$9,733,776
14	Tri-Modal Imager	Mobile passive detection systems with a goal of detection at a distance, 1mC at 100m. The imager has a 2-dimensional active mask and backplane constructed from sodium iodide to provide coded aperture and Compton imaging capability.	Prototype	$7,125,290
15	Integrated Muon Tomography, Gamma and Neutron Detector	Development of a proof of concept system that integrated both gamma detection and muon tomography for the detection of radiological/nuclear material.	Proof of concept	$140,143
16	Target-Linked Radiation Imaging for Standoff Detection	Demonstrate the benefit of fusing target tracking data directly into radiation imaging algorithms by building a target-linked radiation Imaging system that integrates a state-of-the-art video tracking system with advanced cadmium zinc telluride detector technology.		$3,116,158

Domestic Nuclear Detection Office (DNDO) Projects

	Project name	Project description	Product type	Total project costs
17	Advanced Technology Demonstration for Shielded Nuclear Alarm Resolution Program	Development of an active interrogation system for scanning cargo containers with a 9 MeV CW bremsstrahlung photon source capable of detecting high-Z utilizing prompt neutrons from photofission to detect the presence of fissionable material, and nuclear resonance fluorescence to identify isotopic content.	Prototype	$17,541,191
18	Standalone Multiple Anomaly Recognition Technique Advanced Non Intrusive Inspection Algorithm	Development of an image processing algorithm to determine the most likely locations of contraband in radiographic images taken by nonintrusive inspection systems of cargo containers.	Software-algorithms	$1,079,335
19	High Yield Pulsed Neutron Generator	Development of pulsed neutron generator using the deuterium-deuterium reaction with a high average yield and pulse lengths varying from 100 microseconds to 2 microsecond with a fall time of less than 1 microsecond.	Prototype	$1,114,300
20	Intelligent Radiation Sensor System—General Electric	Demonstrate the advanced technologies required to improve the ability to detect, localize, and identify radiological sources by integrating data from multiple portable radiation detectors. In the system, small networked detectors transmit radiation data and their location to a base station, which fuses data from all detectors and determines if detection has occurred. If a source has been detected, the system then uses the available information to locate and identify the source. This information is transmitted back to the user(s) in the array. The system takes into account directional detectors.	Software-algorithms	$8,058,598
21	Intelligent Radiation Sensor System—Passport Systems	Demonstrate the advanced technologies required to improve the ability to detect, localize, and identify radiological sources by integrating data from multiple portable radiation detectors. In this system, small networked detectors coupled with a smart phone processor system. The smart phone is used to gather data from nearby neighbors and perform a local particle filter calculation. These results are passed to the user and the neighboring detectors. If a base station is employed, the results are sent to a base station.	Software-algorithms	$7,832,542
22	Intelligent Radiation Sensor System—Smith Systems	Demonstrate the advanced technologies required to improve the ability to detect, localize, and identify radiological sources by integrating data from multiple portable radiation detectors. In this system, small networked detectors transmit radiation data and their location to a base station, which uses a number of algorithms to determine if detection has occurred. Their primary algorithm is a particle filter. If detection has occurred, the system attempts to location and identify the source using a series of algorithms. This system employs an ultra wide band networking method that allows 3-dimensional positioning in a Global Positioning System-denied environment.	Software-algorithms	$4,900,906

Domestic Nuclear Detection Office (DNDO) Projects

	Project name	Project description	Product type	Total project costs
23	Web-Based Computer Simulation of Radiological Detection Scenario Training	Container Security Initiative will take an existing simulation development tool, assess the feasibility of creating two virtual working detectors, create a new web-based interface where the detectors can be virtually controlled, and establish the web-delivery and administration software specifications for this new approach to training on these instruments.	Software-algorithms	$1,113,500
24	Realistic and Adaptive Interactive Learning System	Propose an innovative approach that brings all of these elements together to develop simulation software that provides physically realistic and effective preventative radiation/nuclear detection training to first responders by first adding radiation transport algorithms to an existing video game engine which will be used to generate training scenarios based on real locations, and then testing the accuracy of those simulations by comparing the virtual environment with data collected from real world measurements.	Software-algorithms	$1,153,254
25	Near Term Replacement for Large Helium-3Tubes	Development and characterization of portal-sized neutron detector modules consisting of layers of 6LiF/ZnS scintillating materials and wavelength shifting fibers.	Prototype	$562,115
26	Development of a 3/6/9 MeV X-ray Generator	Development of a next generation X-ray generator that can deliver photon energies of 3, 6, and 9 MeV in discrete and interleaved modes at a repetition rate of 800-1000 Hertz in the x-band microwave frequency.	Prototype	$1,113,500
27	Neutron Straw-Based Replacement for Advanced Spectroscopic Portal (ASP) and Radiation Portal Monitors(RPM) Helium-3 detectors	Development of portal monitor replacements using boron-coated straw proportional counters embedded in a moderator.	Prototype	$501,075
28	High Sensitivity Detection and Identification of Radiological Threats in Low Scatter-to Clutter Ratio Environments	Develop and demonstrate novel radiological background characterization approaches that will improve the detection capability of both fixed, passive ASP systems, as well as handheld and moviel isotope identifiers. Capability will be directly demonstrated by integrating these algorithms with RadSeeker detector technology. These algorithms will result in the ability to perform clutter suppression yielding de-noised gamma-ray signatures of significantly higher accuracy needed for detection and identification of low activity threats.	Software-algorithms	$466,035
29	Cost Effective Neutron Straw-Based Replacement for ASP and RPM Helium-3 detectors	Development of large diameter boron-coated straws embedded in a moderator as a cost-effective replacement for helium-3 in radiation portal monitors.	Prototype	$442,976

Domestic Nuclear Detection Office (DNDO) Projects

	Project name	Project description	Product type	Total project costs
30	RadMATE - a Mobile RAD/NUC Reachback App	Development of a smart phone application that DNDO calls RadMATE. The vision for RadMATE is to be available to operators in the field primarily to simplify and expedite Reachback, but additionally to provide needed information (e.g. tables to classify sources as innocent or of major concern) and operating procedures when a radiological source is encountered in the field. This will considerably minimize the burden on operators and eliminate the need for a specialized laptop computer with custom Reachback software. It will also ensure that Reachback communications are consistent, complete and more accurate.	Software-algorithms	$168,513
31	Spectroscopic Portal, Active Interrogation, Radiography Threat Alarming	Development of a Smartphone application for radiological threat adjudication to support law enforcement and first responder adjudication of anomalous gamma ray spectra collected on handheld or personal radioisotope identification and spectroscopic personal radiation detector devices.	Software-algorithms	$169,335
32	Non-Radioactive Alternative to Replace Radioactive Sources in Commercial Applications	Design, build, test, and evaluate an engineering prototype neutron generator for Am-Be replacement that is to scale and function to simulate ruggedness and suitability for borehole applications.	Prototype	$817,178
33	Proof of Concept Demonstration of a Compact Accelerator	Research and development to design, build, and demonstrate use of a portable, cost efficient electron accelerator for non-intrusive inspection and verification applications.	Prototype	$1,392,875
34	Bayesian Optimization Algorithm for Automated Spectral Identification of Nuclear Material	Idea is to apply large-scale optimization algorithms (branch and bound) to mixture analysis, use a Bayesian network to incorporate expert knowledge into optimization algorithms, and demonstrate measurable performance gains in RN ID for various detector materials.	Software-Algorithms	$820,593
35	Advanced Technology Research Algorithms for Shielded Nuclear Material Detection	Developing a set of algorithms to locate high-Z material in radiography images	Software-Algorithms	$985,022
36	Study of Fast Neutron Signatures and Measurement Techniques for Shield Nuclear Material (SNM) Detection	Study investigating the benefits of fast vs. thermal neutron signatures for detection of SNM in passive applications; will explore different types of detectors (high pressure He-4, single crystal organic scintillators, and plastics), sources (Cf-252, gamma), backgrounds, and cargos (represented by moderators).	Study	$291,114

Source: DHS.

Table 11:S&T Office of University Programs (OUP) R&D Project Deliverables for Fiscal Years 2010 to 2012

S&T Office of University Programs (OUP) Projects

	Project name	Project description	Product type	Total project costs
1	The Impact on the U.S. Economy of Changes in Wait Times at Ports of Entry	The Impact on the U.S. economy of changes in wait times at ports of entry.	Report	$200,000
2	Analytical Method to Identify the Number of Containers to Inspect at U.S. Ports to Deter Terrorist Attacks	Analytical method to identify the number of containers to inspect at U.S. ports to deter terrorist attacks.	Published report	$80,000
3	Deterring the Smuggling of Nuclear Weapons in Container Freight Through Detection and Retaliation	Deterring the smuggling of nuclear weapons in container freight through detection and retaliation.	Published report	$80,000
4	Application of the Advanced Circulation Coastal Circulation Model for Predicting Near Shore and Inner Shore Transport of Oil from the Horizon Oil Spill	This rapid response project adapted the center's storm surge models to forecast oil landfall during the Gulf Coast Horizon Oil Spill. The work was coordinated with Federal Emergency Management Agency, the National Oceanic and Atmospheric Administration, and the U.S. Army Corps of Engineers.	Report, software, training	$300,000
5	Coast Guard Search and Rescue Visual Analytics	Coast Guard Search and Rescue Visual Analytics–interactive resource allocation tool for search and rescue missions and stations.	Software	$500,000
6	Boat Allocation Module	Boat Allocation Module—operations research resource allocation capability for Coast Guard boat stations.	Software	$150,000
7	Maritime Risk	Risk analysis for maritime traffic in Delaware River.	Report	$600,000
8	Fisheries Law Enforcement	Targeted risk-based decision support tool for Coast Guard operations.	Software	$350,000
9	Migrant Population Characteristics and Flows	This study has sought to develop new statistics that will significantly improve understanding of both the level of legal and illegal immigration through the United States. and the specific demographic attributes of these individuals, and thus enable better informed decision making regarding public services usage, criminal activity, and immigrant assimilation.	Report	$206,000
10	Checkpoint Study	Provides Office of Border Patrol recommendations for improved data collection, performance metrics, community impact assessment and resource allocation tools.	Report	$1,000,000

S&T Office of University Programs (OUP) Projects

11	How Will We Know?: Measures of Border Control	The project's goal is to recommend a —standard for border enforcement effectiveness based on a review of existing research, interviews with Border Patrol and other DHS personnel, and an assessment of the available data.	Analysis/report	$87,875
12	Organization and Networks of Transnational Gangs	The two primary objectives of this study include:(1) further understanding the organizational structure and sophistication of transnational criminal gangs and their capacity to facilitate mobility and migration through Mexico into the United States.; and (2) further understanding the dynamic social networks of transnational criminal gangs and their capacity to facilitate mobility and migration through Mexico into the United States.	Study/report	$228,378
13	Risk-based Allocation of Border Security Assets	The methods and tools offer approaches to allocating border security assets based on criteria of risk. In this project, we asked: what risk-based resource allocation approaches are most effective and how does effectiveness depend on the operational environment.	Study/ report	$224,181
14	Decision Support Systems	Software for data display and fusion was enhanced.	Software	$457,512
15	Satellite Detection and Tracking of Ships and Ice	We have produced near-real-time sea ice imagery and sea ice concentration products. These products are critical aids to operating ships safely in regions where sea ice (and potentially marine mammals) represent hazards.	Prototype	
16	Ship Detection using Multi/Hyperspectral Images	Analysis of imagery and development of software for sensor information and anomaly detections.	Software/report	
17	Satellite Detection and Tracking of Ships	Software for constellation optimization was developed and evaluated.	Software	$851,000
18	PROTECT: Port Resilience Operational Tactical Enforcement to Combat Terrorism	Randomized inspection scheduling tool for Coast Guard surveillance operations.	Software	$813,845[a]

Source: DHS.

[a]This project was co-funded between OUP grant monies and RDC RDT&E funding. RDC is the USCG Project Manager and obtained support from OUP COEs using Basic Ordering Agreement task orders to develop and test software prototype. OUP contr bution to software development is complete. However, USCG PROTECT software development and testing is ongoing.

Appendix I: Department of Homeland Security
(DHS) Border and Maritime List of Completed
and Discontinued Research and Development
(R&D) Project Deliverables for Fiscal Years
2010 through 2012

Table 12: List of DHS Discontinued Border and Maritime R&D Projects for Fiscal Years 2010 through 2012

Science and Technology Directorate (S&T) Borders and Maritime Security Division (BMD)

	Project name	Reason for discontinuation	Project costs[a]
1	Border and Maritime Systems Basic Research	Reduced funding and strategic move to reduce basic research	Not Available
2	Complex Systems Analysis and Basic Research	Reduced funding and strategic move to reduce basic research	Not Available
3	Can Scan	Stopped at preliminary review due to lack of CBP acquisition funding	$13 million
4	Safe Container	Reduced funding in fiscal year 2012	$20 million

Domestic Nuclear Detection Office (DNDO)

1	Mapping isotopic distributions in cargo (FINDER) to detect Special Nuclear Material and its configuration	Technology found not feas ble	$4,780,427
2	Directed-Radiation for Active-Interrogation near Coastal Cities	Technology found not feas ble	$2,190,600
3	Shielded Nuclear Alarm Resolution System	Technology found not feas ble	$7,462,370
4	Intensity-Modulated Advanced X-Ray Source	Technology found not feas ble	Not Available
5	A Fast Pulse, Portable Neutron Source for Special Nuclear Materials Detection	Technology found not feas ble	$557,143
6	Demonstration of Close Proximity Gravity Detection for Shielded Fissile Materials in Vessels	Technology found not feas ble	$440,229

S&T Office of University Programs (OUP)

1	Reduction of False Alarm Rates	Data not provided by DHS at sector/headquarters level – Principle Investigator (PI) did not make progress in finding alternate testing data.	Not Available
2	Fusion of Spatial-Temporal Sensor Data	PI did not make progress—lack of adequate funding	Not Available
3	Dynamic Resource Allocation Using Market-based Methods	PI did not make progress—lack of adequate funding	Not Available
4	Border Security Risk Assessment and Maturity Model	PI did not make progress	Not Available
5	K-12 Summer Seminar Camps	Discontinued by OUP Program Manager as focus shifted to higher education	Not Available
6	Maritime Domain Awareness Curricular Sequence	Discontinued by OUP Program Manager as focus shifted to higher education	Not Available
7	Preparing Rural and Alaska Native Students for DHS Careers	Discontinued by OUP Program Manager as focus shifted to higher education	Not Available
8	Advanced High Frequency Radar Design: An integrative Approach of Novel Antennas, Propagation Modeling, and Digital Signal Processing Performance Optimization Algorithms	Discontinued by Center for Island, Maritime, and Extreme Environment Security (CIMES) Director when antennas seemed unlikely candidates for transition to stakeholders.	Not Available
9	Project 2.1: Resiliency Modeling	Insufficient funding	Not Available

Appendix I: Department of Homeland Security
(DHS) Border and Maritime List of Completed
and Discontinued Research and Development
(R&D) Project Deliverables for Fiscal Years
2010 through 2012

Science and Technology Directorate (S&T) Borders and Maritime Security Division (BMD)

	Project name	Reason for discontinuation	Project costs[a]
10	Project 2.2: Resilient and Cognitive Port Infrastructure Systems and Enterprises	Insufficient funding	Not Available
11	Estimates of the Unauthorized Population and Visa Overstays	PI opted out	Not Available
12	Effective Bi-national Border Security Governance	No progress made towards tangible outcomes	Not Available
13	CIMES Summer Undergraduate Research Program and Visiting Faculty	Discontinued by OUP Program Manager as focus shifted to higher education	Not Available
14	Pattern Analyses from Remote Sensing Data	Reason for discontinuation not provided	Not Available
15	Detection and Tracking of Hidden Objects	Reason for discontinuation not provided	Not Available
16	Wireless Sensor Network Development	Reason for discontinuation not provided	Not Available
17	Sensor Fusion for Intent and Hotspot Detection	Reason for discontinuation not provided	Not Available
18	Vehicle Detection, Identification and Screening	Reason for discontinuation not provided	Not Available
19	Extended Battery Life for Sensor Networks	Reason for discontinuation not provided	Not Available

Source: DHS.

[a]Due to the nature of funding of R&D and grant funding, individual project costs were not readily available.

Appendix II: Comments from the Department of Homeland Security

U.S. Department of Homeland Security
Washington, DC 20528

 Homeland
Security

September 13, 2013

David C. Maurer
Director, Homeland Security and Justice Issues
U.S. Government Accountability Office
441 G Street, NW
Washington, DC 20548

Re: Draft Report GAO-13-732, "DEPARTMENT OF HOMELAND SECURITY:
Opportunities Exist to Better Evaluate and Coordinate Border and Maritime Research and
Development"

Dear Mr. Maurer:

Thank you for the opportunity to review and comment on this draft report. The U.S. Department
of Homeland Security (DHS) appreciates the U.S. Government Accountability Office's (GAO's)
work in planning and conducting its review and issuing this report.

The DHS Science and Technology (S&T) Directorate mission is to strengthen America's
security and resiliency by providing knowledge products and innovative technology solutions for
the Homeland Security Enterprise (HSE). S&T does this by:

- *focusing operationally* by providing the HSE with strategic and focused technology
  options and operational process enhancements,

- *providing innovative* systems-based solutions to complex homeland security problems,
  and

- *building partnerships* with the technical depth and reach to discover, adapt, and leverage
  technology solutions developed by federal agencies and laboratories; state, local, and
  tribal governments; and the private sector—across the United States and internationally.

The draft report contained two recommendations, with which DHS concurs. Specifically, GAO
recommended that the Secretary of Homeland Security instruct the Under Secretary for Science
and Technology to:

Recommendation 1: Establish timeframes and milestones for collecting and evaluating
feedback from its customers to determine the usefulness and impact of its R&D projects and
deliverables, and use it to make better-informed decisions regarding future work.

Response: Concur. In support of its mission to provide knowledge products and innovative technology solutions for the HSE, S&T's project managers, as a standard business practice, routinely seek and provide opportunities to gather customer feedback during project execution. Timely and pertinent situational awareness on all projects is ensured by encouraging customers to participate in design reviews, prototype tests, and demonstrations for the expressed purpose of gathering feedback for current development projects. For example, when prototypes are first fielded, they are typically operated by customers (i.e., end-users, not developers) in operational settings for extended periods of time. User feedback is sought and modifications are made on the basis of customer experiences and the refinement of operational requirements.

Feedback to guide future work is also gathered at the DHS S&T annual portfolio review, which includes stakeholders and customers. S&T is also developing R&D Strategies with DHS Components and will update them annually on the basis of customer feedback. In addition, by March 31, 2014, all S&T project plans will be modified to include a milestone requiring formalized feedback from its customers. This milestone will be tied to a significant project event (e.g., Go/No Decisions, Test, Deliverable/Transition, etc.), but will be completed at least annually. The feedback obtained will be used to make better informed decisions for the associated project and future R&D efforts.

S&T has also established and is implementing a Project Management Guide to enhance overall project management at all stages of development. As recognized in the draft GAO report, a Customer Survey Template is included as an appendix in the Guide. This survey will be completed by customers at the conclusion of the project to inform future R&D projects. Estimated Completion Date (ECD): September 30, 2014.

Recommendation 2: Ensure that design limitations with regard to data reliability, accessibility, and availability are reviewed and understood before approving Center of Excellence R&D projects.

Response: Concur. DHS agrees it should carefully consider potential data needs, access issues, and data limitations before approving Center of Excellence (COE) projects and S&T's Office of University Programs has already made significant strides to strengthen efforts in this regard. For example, its current standard practice is to restrict project funding until the COEs submit detailed work plans and requisite supporting materials, including the agreement of a DHS Component to provide any required support personnel, facilities, or data.

To further facilitate the COEs' access to DHS information, including investigator-initiated projects, S&T is working to develop standard guidelines and protocols that would apply universally to all COEs. These protocols will describe how data sets must be modified to enable their use in open-source, unrestricted research formats by making anonymous specific references to individuals, locations, demographic characteristics, or law enforcement issues. To improve information access, S&T is also encouraging COEs to voluntarily convene workshops that will engage both researchers and DHS Components to better understand constraints to and develop protocols for acquiring and using government data. ECD: September 30, 2014.

2

Again, thank you for the opportunity to review and comment on this draft report. Technical comments were previously provided under separate cover. Please feel free to contact me if you have any questions. We look forward to working with you in the future.

Sincerely,

Jim H. Crumpacker
Director
Departmental GAO-OIG Liaison Office

3

Appendix III: GAO Contact and Staff Acknowledgments

GAO Contact	David C. Maurer, (202) 512-9627 or maurerd@gao.gov
Staff Acknowledgments	In addition to the contact named above, Chris Currie (Assistant Director), Aditi Archer, Charlotte Gamble, and Gary Malavenda made key contributions to this report, and Michele Fejfar, Robert Fletcher, and Richard Hung assisted with design and methodology. Frances Cook provided legal support. Jessica Orr and Eric Hauswirth provided assistance in report preparation.

GAO's Mission	The Government Accountability Office, the audit, evaluation, and investigative arm of Congress, exists to support Congress in meeting its constitutional responsibilities and to help improve the performance and accountability of the federal government for the American people. GAO examines the use of public funds; evaluates federal programs and policies; and provides analyses, recommendations, and other assistance to help Congress make informed oversight, policy, and funding decisions. GAO's commitment to good government is reflected in its core values of accountability, integrity, and reliability.
Obtaining Copies of GAO Reports and Testimony	The fastest and easiest way to obtain copies of GAO documents at no cost is through GAO's website (http://www.gao.gov). Each weekday afternoon, GAO posts on its website newly released reports, testimony, and correspondence. To have GAO e-mail you a list of newly posted products, go to http://www.gao.gov and select "E-mail Updates."
Order by Phone	The price of each GAO publication reflects GAO's actual cost of production and distribution and depends on the number of pages in the publication and whether the publication is printed in color or black and white. Pricing and ordering information is posted on GAO's website, http://www.gao.gov/ordering.htm. Place orders by calling (202) 512-6000, toll free (866) 801-7077, or TDD (202) 512-2537. Orders may be paid for using American Express, Discover Card, MasterCard, Visa, check, or money order. Call for additional information.
Connect with GAO	Connect with GAO on Facebook, Flickr, Twitter, and YouTube. Subscribe to our RSS Feeds or E-mail Updates. Listen to our Podcasts. Visit GAO on the web at www.gao.gov.
To Report Fraud, Waste, and Abuse in Federal Programs	Contact: Website: http://www.gao.gov/fraudnet/fraudnet.htm E-mail: fraudnet@gao.gov Automated answering system: (800) 424-5454 or (202) 512-7470
Congressional Relations	Katherine Siggerud, Managing Director, siggerudk@gao.gov, (202) 512-4400, U.S. Government Accountability Office, 441 G Street NW, Room 7125, Washington, DC 20548
Public Affairs	Chuck Young, Managing Director, youngc1@gao.gov, (202) 512-4800 U.S. Government Accountability Office, 441 G Street NW, Room 7149 Washington, DC 20548

Please Print on Recycled Paper.